ELDERSHIP DEVELOPMENT
FROM APPLICATION TO AFFIRMATION

About the Backstage Pastors Book Series

The Backstage Pastors series of books have been designed to target specific topics with enough depth to provide meaningful direction but with a brevity that facilitates reading or skimming quickly. My hope is to put extremely practical tools into your hands at a reasonable cost that will quickly *train you up* so that you are quickly *freed up* to continue with the demands of life and ministry.

I've chosen to publish these books on Amazon for multiple reasons. One key driver is that this platform allows me the freedom to regularly tweak, update and expand these works. In essence, the book never has to be done. With that in mind, I invite you to take notes and send me your thoughts at backstagepastors@gmail.com. Who knows, maybe the next edition will include your insight or question!

Find information about my pastoral coaching, consulting and speaking, as well as new articles on practical topics at www.backstagepastors.com. Continue the conversation online by using #backstagepastors.

ELDERSHIP DEVELOPMENT
FROM APPLICATION TO AFFIRMATION

PHIL TAYLOR

Floodlight Press
Orlando, Florida

Copyright © 2017 by Phil Taylor
First Edition
1.2

All rights reserved. No part of this book may be reproduced, stored in a retrieval system, or transmitted in any form by any means, electronic, mechanical, photocopy, recording, or otherwise, without the prior permission of the publisher, except for the inclusion of brief quotations in review, without prior permission in writing from the author/publisher.

All scripture quotations, unless otherwise indicated, are taken from the HOLY BIBLE, ENGLISH STANDARD VERSION®. ESV®. Copyright © 2002 by Crossway. All rights reserved.

Page layout and e-book: Lisa Parnell, lparnell.com

Floodlight Press
Orlando, Florida

ASIN: B06VS6H7VD
ISBN-13: 978-0-9987182-0-0
ISBN-10: 0998718203

Dedication

I would like to dedicate this book to my dad,
F. Stuart Taylor.

He served the church vocationally for over 50 years. If I know anything about leadership in the church, I learned it first by watching him *love* the church.

There is a phrase that I've heard him say many times when it comes to church governance: "If the men leading your church are *godly*, it doesn't really make much difference what you call them. If the men leading your church are *un-godly*, it doesn't really make much difference what you call them." Thanks for leading me well Dad!

Profits from This Book

More than anything else I've written or plan to write, this book is a collection of tools gathered from many places. Some origins are lost to time and memory. Almost all of it was developed or collected directly for the churches I've worked at while being paid by them. As such, I did not feel right profiting from this book in any way. So I've decided to give 100% of the profits to missionary friends serving refugees that are pouring into Europe as I write this. If you'd like more information on them, feel free to email me at backstagepastors@gmail.com.

Contents

Acknowledgments — ix

Introduction — 1

Step One: Surfacing Potential Elders — 9

Step Two: The Prerequisites to Entering the Elder Development Process — 17

Step Three: The Application and Post Application Meeting — 25

Step Four: Year One of the Elder Development Collective — 45

Step Five: Year Two of the Elder Development Collective — 55

Step Six: The Post Development Process Checklist Form — 67

Step Seven: The Final Meeting Before Public Affirmation — 81

Step Eight: Public Affirmation — 85

Conclusion — 87

Appendix One: Covenant Partnership *at* Mosaic Church — 89

Appendix Two: Elders/Pastors Covenant *with* Mosaic Church — 97

Appendix Three: Our Elder Teams Experiment — 101

Appendix Four: How to get everything you see here in a word file. — 109

Endnotes — 111

Bibliography and Resources on Biblical Eldership — 113

Acknowledgments

This book exists because I've gotten to do leadership development in several church contexts. I'm grateful for experimental spaces like King's Chapel, Terra Nova Church and Mosaic Church. It was at these churches where this material was slowly developed—usually with the help of others. I'd also like to thank those individuals who helped make this book a reality. My editor, Jimmy Hoang, my graphic designer and web consultant Keith Winter. And of course, my fellow church leaders at Mosaic, who saw fit to allow me to step away from the office for a week on a writing retreat to get the bulk of this work done. I'm grateful to be a part of a church that values serving and resourcing other churches.

> "Whether formal or informal, recognized or unrecognized, leadership is a given in any church. In fact, leadership is a given in any human society."
> — ROBERT H. THUNE[1]

Introduction

Why did I bother to write this book?

It's really quite simple. Churches need spiritual leaders to *actively shepherd* the congregation. The Bible gives us some clear definition for the character and skill set of these leaders and calls them Elders (or Pastors, Bishops, Shepherds and Overseers interchangeably). Until relatively recently, there were not many resources to help make sense of what we find in Scripture. Then, in the 1990's Alexander Strauch wrote his groundbreaking call to arms titled *Biblical Eldership: An Urgent Call to Restore Biblical Church Leadership*. I think it is safe to say that this one book has had more influence on the restoration and expansion of Elder qualified leadership than any other extra-biblical work before or since. In many ways, it is *the textbook* for Eldership in the church.

Over the years, about 25 other books have been published on the role and work of the Elder. Many of them are incredibly useful at helping people think through the "Elder Model" of church leadership. Most of them give a few practical and helpful tips for implementation at your church. Several study guides have been made to help groups or individuals think through the importance of becoming an Elder, the biblical support for Eldership, and the related theological discussions that must take place. This incredible body of work that has been developed over the last twenty years assists pastors and leaders in understanding the *theory* behind Biblical Eldership and the *daily practice* of those Elders.

So, why then did I find myself receiving emails constantly (like, 5-6 times a month) asking me if I could share my documents from the Eldership Development Process that I "created" for my church in Florida? (I used quote marks around the word "created" because I feel more like a curator of various tools I've acquired over the years.) From my perspective, the process we were using felt simple and straightforward and kind of obvious. Yet, the emails kept coming. I finally realized that despite all the great theoretical and theological books arguing for the Elder Model and the study guides teaching Elders how to "Eld", as one pastor friend calls it, there was a shocking lack of writing describing the actual process of developing Elders from start to finish—from *application* straight through to *affirmation*.[2]

Sometimes, you just need to see how one church does something from start to finish in order to figure out how you want to do it at your church. You may not like some of the process decisions that our church makes, but at least you have a starting point as you develop something of your own. Given that you are a unique creation called to lead your specific church in a particular culture and context, I would hope that you would look at the process I've developed and say "we'll need to mess with this a bit for it to work at our church." That's the spirit with which this book has been *assembled*. Again, I hesitate to describe what I'm doing here as "writing" because this is such an amalgamation of things I've picked up over the years.

Think of this more like a case study. This is not a book that tells you *how you must do it*. Rather, this is a book that explains *how we did it*. Or at least, it tells you how we do it right now, this year. In fact, after taking tons of guys through a robust two-year

Elder Development Process, I saw some gaps and opportunities for improvement. Writing this book forced me to put those adjustments down on paper. You will no doubt want to contextualize it for your setting. You can expect a 2nd Edition at some point in the future because I'm 100% certain that we have not figured this out perfectly. In fact, I'm probably already making little course corrections that cause the book you are holding to be slightly out of date. That's the nature of ministry in a constantly changing world. You will always need leaders, but the variant ways that you develop them are infinite.

Please Tell Me You've Read Other Books on Eldership Already?

With this emphasis on how *one church* did it, I desperately hope that this book is not your starting point in studying Biblical Eldership. Go read Alexander Strauch's book first (at least the 47 page version of it). Seriously, I'm not joking. You really don't want to start here. Go get the theory first, then come back for the process. Just please understand that I will spend very little time explaining what the Bible says about Eldership, or the theology behind it. I won't deal in depth with gender issues, or Greek and Hebrew words or the difference between Elders and Deacons or the interchangeableness of the titles Elder, Pastor, Bishop, Overseer and Shepherd. I will *assume* that you have read other books on the subject, and you've turned to this book because you are ready to build a process for your church. Take whatever you want from here. Use it, mess with it, change it, steal it, restate it, call it your own. I really don't care what you do with what you find here. My simple goal is to give you a tool to use to develop better Elders in your church context. That's it.

So you won't tell me what the Bible says about Elders?

Actually no, that's not the focus of this book. This is a systems and process book, not a theory and biblical exposition book. That said, you *will* see our church's beliefs on the role of Elder bleed through on many pages. So it's worth taking just a minute to give you a rough sketch of what we believe about Elders.

We want Elders that are biblically qualified to actively shepherd the people of our church. We are a staff-operated, elder-guided church. Some of our Elders are on staff, most are not. The primary task of our Elders is to be deeply involved in the spiritual care and development of those who call Mosaic Church home. I say to our men all the time, "Your job is to shepherd the people of Mosaic, occasionally, that might involve making a decision." As such, Elder meetings are not a critical part of our rhythm. We keep our Elders *informed* of decisions, but they are rarely *involved* in every little decision unless it touches their area of involvement in the church. Our Elders are aware the finances and have the freedom to speak up, but only really do so when things are going awry. The staff (which has several Elders on it) hire and fire staff, decide budgets, do small capital projects, make ministry decisions and generally run the day to day operations of the church all without the need for full Elder approval. We just don't see that as the job of our Elders. Again, they are not board members. They are active shepherds.[3]

Yet, there are times when we say, "this decision should go to the Elders". It includes some obvious things like doctrinal disputes, major spiritual/moral issues with key staff, the big vision for the churches future and the largest ramifications of that vision. For example, our Elders would need to sign off on a large loan for a new building. They would be involved in deciding where to plant our next campus or in hiring a new Lead Pastor. But they would not be the ones to decide if we should repaint the Adult Education classrooms, or spend the money to get our Discipleship Pastor an executive assistant, or upgrade the sound system in the sanctuary.

The reality is that Staff Elders *are* involved in almost all of these types of decisions, but the difference is that in our context, we do not require some sort of "board approval" before moving forward on every little thing. If at any point a decision is made that an Elder disagrees with, he has the freedom to come forward an express that disagreement in the right forum. In that sense, an involved Elder who is actively-shepherding will always be in a place of "guarding the church."

So to summarize here: throughout this book, you will see that I am not training up a board of directors whose job it is to pour over P & L sheets. I am training up a group of men who can actively shepherd those who call Mosaic Church home.

Will This Work In My Smaller Church Context?

I serve in a multi-site mega-church in Florida called Mosaic. Statistically speaking, you probably are not in very large church like ours and might wonder if this will work in your smaller context. Here's the thing—that's a valid concern—but I have not been at Mosaic forever. In fact, half of my ministry career to date has been spent in churches under 500 in average attendance. Plus, the multi-site nature of our mega-church has meant that I have had a role in leading one large church and multiple smaller churches at the very same time! The Elder Development system you are about to discover has worked well in our largest campus as well as our smaller campuses. We are developing Elders across the whole church at all times. The key difference for you is that you may not have someone on your staff like me who can put a ton of time into developing a system like this ... *which is exactly why I've put it in book form! So that you don't have to re-invent the wheel!* What I've done here in this book would have worked just fine in every church I've been a part of. So, put the "size context" concern away. This will work if you are training one person at a time or a hundred people all at once.

How should I Use This Book?

As Research: You probably won't love everything about this book. I'm unique. You're unique. Our churches are unique. It's fine. Use it to inform what you build in your church context. In that case, treat this book like a case-study. Pick and choose what you like and build your own system. Hopefully, reading this will save you some time and allow you to start out running, rather than walking.

As Your System: Pastors are busy people. Do you really want or have the time to create your own application, reading schedules, etc? If you need a system right away, you could literally take exactly what I've done and use it at your church, swapping out the word "Mosaic" for your church name and altering the schedules to fit your reality, or replacing one of the books with something different that you prefer. I want to make that easy for you. I don't want you to have to type all this stuff up again. So if you email me at backstagepastors@gmail.com, I will literally send you every tool you are about to see in a format that is totally editable. I write practical things for pastors to use. I don't care what you do with it after that. Time is short and the church needs leaders, so let's work together. My goal is that in under a day or two, you could be ready to implement this system in your church. And since you'd have the Word files (see Appendix 4), you can alter it over time to be contextually appropriate, and let it take on a life of it's own at your church. All I ask is that you don't sell it or republish it.

Make It Better: I've tried to make it clear in this intro that what you are reading is a work in progress. If you make an alteration in your church context that you find to be extremely effective, please email me about that. I may add your suggestion into the next edition of this book or post about it on my website, backstagepastors.com. Let's learn from each other!

How Is the Book Laid Out?

From here on out, every chapter is a step in our process. To get a quick overview, flip back to the table of contents. In each chapter, I will intro the step and then tell you and show you exactly what I do with our Elders In Process. Everything set apart within borders is exactly what I send out to people going through our process. Throughout the book, you will see call outs labeled *"Notes for the Implementor"* where I'll take time to explain the line of thinking behind some aspect of the process. If you have questions that I'm not answering in the text, email them to me so that I can make the next edition of this book better.

Enjoy!

> "Better a godly elder with mediocre leadership gifts than a charismatic leader with glaring moral flaws"
> — JEREMY RINNE[4]

Surfacing Potential Elders

Finding Them

In order to train up Elders, you have to actually find a few guys that you think might be potential Elder material. There are a number of ways this can be done. Some churches will simply go and ask men to serve on the Elder team for a season. This works well if your Elders are essentially board members who gather to make decisions. But if you want your Elders to function as highly trained, highly committed shepherd/pastors (we call it "active shepherding"), then you are going to want them to have a sense a "calling" to it. Paul tells us that it is good to "aspire to the role of Elder" (1 Timothy 3:1). Personally speaking, I want our Elders to *want* to be an Elder/Pastor, I don't want someone doing me or the church a favor. This isn't the PTA, or your kids soccer league in need of *just one more coach*. This is a big deal, and it's going to raise the stakes in the Elders life and family.

If he is on staff, he steps out of whatever org chart exists on paper and into a plurality of equals charged with the spiritual care of the church. If he is a lay Elder, he will find his free time a little less free. He will have to say no to other opportunities in order to have time for active-shepherding each week. You can't very well "ask" someone if they would be willing to be an Elder and then "tell" them to step into a two-year intensive process like the one I've built here. But if someone comes to you and says "I think God might be calling me to be an Elder, what do you think?" then you have the ability to call them into some intensive training.

However, if your church does not have a track record of training up Elders, and you've never done any teaching from the pulpit on biblical leadership, then no one will actually know that they should "step up" and say "I think I might be an Elder." In fact, you'll have some awesome guys who will hold back thinking that it would be prideful or arrogant or presumptuous to "want to be an Elder."

When we first introduced a more robust training program for new Elders at Mosaic, we kicked it off with a sermon on leadership in the church where we talked about Deacons and Elders, what they do and what the training looks like for each. Out of that one weekend, I had twenty-two men express an interest in Eldership. Seventeen of them actually made it through the application process, several dropped out in the first year (not all by choice), and several more never quite made it to the finish line. In the end, we had twelve come out of that one sermon and finish the Eldership Development Process, and they are all actively shepherding at Mosaic as I write. The process worked in part because every one of them wanted it bad enough to do the work.

So if this is brand new in your church, consider teaching a sermon on biblical leadership. You could combine it with another sermon on biblical community and another on membership or covenant partnership (everyone has a different name for this). If you do this near the beginning of the year, you could kick it off with a vision sermon, followed by three sermons that essentially unpack how this family does life together to create a nice month long series (check out ours online[5]). Once you've established a leadership development culture, word will get out, and you won't have to constantly give people permission to come forward.

Vetting Them

Right about now, some of you have a face in mind. It's that super annoying guy in your church that you would never in a million years put into leadership, but if someone says in a sermon, "It's OK to aspire to be an Elder," he'll be emailing you from his smartphone *during church* to let you know that he is ready to report for duty.... Yup, that's going to happen.... Several times in fact.... And your going to have to take a deep breath and deal with him and the others who think they should be Elders but either can't be or shouldn't be for various reasons.

This is why it is so important that you only dole out the steps of the Eldership process a little bit at a time. Don't post your whole process on your website. Keep it kinda secret. (Shoot, I probably shouldn't have written a book about ours and published it for all the world to see?!) This forces a face-to-face meeting with all those aspiring to Eldership. We made the mistake of posting the application as a form on our internal Church Community Builder page thinking it would be easier to manage that way. It didn't take long before an odd dude filled it out and started telling people that he was in the Eldership Development Process. *He wasn't.*

So before you give anyone the application or even the list of pre-requisites, you need to first decide if this person has *any* potential to become an Elder. I'm not saying you check his references and doctrine and everything else at this point, I just mean that if you already know that this guy probably shouldn't be an Elder right now, don't get his hopes up or waste his time with a bunch of work just because you don't have the guts to tell him he's not ready to be an Elder. Be truthful about your perception of his trajectory of growth and development.

In many cases, the people who come forward expressing an interest in Eldership are some of your absolute best people in the church. I often find myself responding this way, "I was wondering when you were going to step up. I've wanted you on an Elder Team for years!" For people like this, you can decide whether or not you want to skip right to the list of pre-requisites found in Step Two. I keep mine on an Evernote file on my phone and computer which allows me to simply text or email the link to the list. (Don't worry, it's in a later chapter here as well).

The First Face-To-Face Meeting

Regardless of what happens with a persons' process, you really need a face-to-face meeting, even if you know you are going to reject him before he even gets started. If I know that I need to gently turn a guy down, I go into the meeting with a prayed up strategy and hope that he takes it well. I don't want to do that via email. I want to shepherd this guy face-to-face through the reasons why he is not qualified to be an Elder, or why he is not ready to be an Elder right now. It is best if one Elder is the gate-keeper for all of these initial meetings. In smaller churches, that will likely be the Lead Pastor. In larger churches, it may be the Executive Pastor or Discipleship Pastor. It probably ought to be the person who oversees the Elder Development Process because he will gain the ability to know instinctively if someone should or should not be an Elder or is not ready to be an Elder.

But enough about rejection—you want to do a face-to-face meeting with all who express an interest in Eldership because it gives you a chance to sit and hear that persons heart for ministry. Let me suggest a few questions and talking points to help guide your first meeting:

Questions For Your First Meeting

Ask a few questions about work and family to gauge general bandwidth for Eldership. If he talks about how stressed he is at work, or how the travel has been so crazy lately, or how marriage seems to be a struggle right now, you will probably need to shift gears into counseling mode and then explain that this sounds like it's not the best time to step into a time intensive Elder Development Process. Encourage him to come back to you when life settles down a bit.

Ask him about the journey to this place of desiring the role of Elder? How did the Spirit lead him in this? What does his wife think? You are just trying to see what is going on in his heart. You are looking for the motive. It doesn't need to be perfect, but it should not be glaringly evil. You want to hear answers like "I've always had this sense that I should be in church leadership, but I never knew what to do with that until the Pastor taught that sermon last month." You don't want to hear things like "I'm concerned about the direction of our church, and I want to be a part of changing it." RED FLAG! This guy has his own vision for the church, and it's probably not the one the Elders collectively agreed to last year and had printed on T-shirts. "I've always wanted to learn biblical doctrine" tells you that he may not need or want to be an Elder, he just wants to learn theology. That's a different class or book that you can point him to. "I really love praying for people and coming alongside them in hard times". Ding, Ding, Ding, Ding, Ding! You struck gold! Get this guy a list of pre-reqs fast! He'll lift *hours* of counseling off your plate and love doing it!

Ask him what he thinks an Elder does? Often times, people misunderstand the role or purpose of an Elder. By listening to what he imagines an Elder does, you gain a sense of why he was drawn to it in the first place. Again, you are really just trying to catch his spiritual heartbeat. I usually talk here about our "active shepherding model" vs. a "board of directors model". (See the appendix on Elder Teams).

Ask him to talk about the people or places where he is already serving and shepherding. A shepherd can't help but shepherd people. It's in his blood. The best Elders are the ones that are already Elder-ing and decide to just make it official (but resist the temptation to fast track these guys, it will come back to bite you, trust me!) If a guy wants to be an Elder at your church, but he has never really been involved before this moment even though he's been a part of the church for awhile, he's not ready. Period. He may be looking for power without all the messiness of dealing with people. Direct him to start leading a small group, or serving with kids ministry for awhile. Anything really. He just needs to prove that he really does have a servant's heart. Use this as a coaching/shepherding moment for him. If the guy can't tell you where he is already serving because he's really new, this is a chance to push him into getting to know the church better by first serving in other ways before shooting for the top spot. Making someone brand new in your church a full Elder is like making the college intern the Lead Pastor just because he's super excited and has a lot of free time. When people are new in a church, they think everything is great. Let him see your churches faults first. Tarnish and temper his view of your church just enough to see if he sticks around.

Explain the extensive nature of the Elder Development Process and ask if he thinks he can handle that right now? I usually give them a thumbnail sketch of the process like this "There is a list of prerequisites that might involve some work. Then, you fill out a really long and invasive application that will feel like a colonoscopy on your spiritual life. Some guys tell me that it took them ten hours to fill it out. Then we gather a couple of Elders with you and your wife to discuss your application. Then, Year One and Two of the Eldership Development Collective finally begins. You will read literally thousands of pages of doctrine and other books. The focus is on learning in the first year and active shepherding in the second year. It will be busy. At then end of two years, we ask you to fill out a form you fill out that asks if you actually did all the work you said you'd do. If you didn't, we wait for you to finish before moving you forward. If all goes well, you finally become a full Elder and are affirmed on stage. This is at least a two-year process. Most people find that it takes them two and a half years by the time they figure in the prerequisites and the application. Are you up for something like this?" I want to be honest with people up front about the workload and give them the chance to gracefully back away.

Moving Them Onto the Next Step

Do you get the impression that I'm trying to scare people away from Eldership and find any reason to not push a guy forward? That's kind of true. I want our Elder team to be like the Marine Seals, the best of the best of the best. These are the guys I want fighting beside me in a battle. So, yes, I take the vetting process pretty seriously. But I also know that there are a number of places for someone to fall out of the process ahead, so if I think a guy "might" have what it takes, I encourage him to move forward and then I just wait to see if he does. And of course, I make it clear that at any point in this 2+ year process, either one of us can back out. The guy can say "Hey, this isn't for me", and I or the Elders can say "We love you, but this isn't for you." Make it clear that going through the process does not guarantee an Elder position.

After this initial face-to-face meeting, I give him the list of pre-requisites (assuming things went well). In fact, I'll often pull it up on my phone during the first meeting if I think it's going well, and I'll walk through the list and then I text or email it to him right then and there. I usually say something definitive like, "Ok, well, the ball is in your court now, I'll wait for you to tell me that you've done the pre-reqs." And then I do nothing to follow up with him. Literally nothing. If he lets it sit for six months—that tells me that he does not have time to move forward. If he brings it up awkwardly in the lobby, "I still need to finish up that list, sorry about that" then I either let him off the hook or challenge him to man up. "Hey it's OK, it's a lot of work—that list. You know, maybe this is just a busy time for you? It's Ok to feel like you are supposed to be an Elder, but realize that you need to wait until you finish your masters degree, or get your kids out of diapers or whatever. Sometimes God puts a call on your life but does not tell you the timeline." Or sometimes it sounds like this: "You and I both know you are supposed to do this, but it's going to be hard work. You are going to have to decide if you are willing to sacrifice other parts of your life in order to become an Elder." Every situation is different.

Let's move onto Step Two, The Prerequisites to Entering the Eldership Development Process.

> "The saying is trustworthy: If anyone aspires to the office of overseer, he desires a noble task."
>
> —1 TIMOTHY 3:1 ESV

The Prerequisites to Entering the Elder Development Process

Before a person can enter the Elder Development process they need to be able to meet certain prerequisites. While this *does* serve the purpose of creating a "hoop", it is also the key to using your leadership development time wisely.

As explained in the previous chapter, I have found that giving out the prerequisites to those who may not make the best Elders is pre-mature and may come back to haunt you at a later time. I have also found that this list must be separate from everything else. I used to include it along with the application and the first year reading list and schedule, essentially giving everyone everything to get started all at once, as long as I was inviting them into the process. What I found was that in a rush to start on time, potential Elders would skip a prerequisite, or jump right to the application and start filling that out. The next time I would see them would be the post-application meeting, and I would not always remember to ask them about the prerequisites.

So I created this checklist that I email or text to people once I tell them to go ahead and move forward. I like to put these files on Evernote and use the share feature where you can actually create a link that you share out to others. No need to log into anything. And if I email someone the list today, I can change it at anytime, and the next time they click on the link, they get the most recent version. It's like a mini-webpage that only the people you give it to can access. By giving people *bite size amounts* of the process at a time, they are able to focus more and see what you need them to see right then.

There are some things in your church that are non-negotiables for your Elders. Your list may be different than ours. There may be some class that everyone in your church must go through. There may be an event that defines your church calendar that you want all Elders at, or a sermon series that shapes your whole philosophy. Whatever is incredibly important in the life of your church ought to be pre-requisite experiences for your potential Elders.

You'll note that I reference another meeting here to be scheduled after someone does the prerequisites. Truthfully, I rarely do that meeting. But there are times when someone indicates a desire to be an Elder and while I'm not 100% comfortable with him, I'm not ready to shut him down either. In those cases, I may go ahead and give him the pre-requisites list knowing that either he'll look at it and not measure up, or he'll see the reading requirement and never get around to finishing. But occasionally, one of these types of guys surprises me and comes back saying "It took me two months but I got everything done on that list of prerequisites." For that guy, I want to take a second look, face-to-face, and see what I find. But again, in many cases, if I have no concern about moving forward, I usually just say "We don't need to meet again. I'll just send you the application, and you can get started on that next."

On the following pages, you will find exactly what I send out in the pre-requisite link.

Step Two: The Prerequisites to Entering the Elder Development Process

Thanks for expressing interest in becoming an Elder at Mosaic Church. The Scriptures tell us that when we desire to be an Elder, we desire a good thing! (1 Tim. 3:1) Before we go any further in this journey, we need to check in on a few things. Take a look at the list below. If you can check every box here in the affirmative, let's set up a meeting! You can do that by emailing my assistant.

— *Phil Taylor, Executive Pastor of Leadership and Development*

☐ Do you believe that you meet the 1 Timothy 3 requirements for elders/pastors? As a reminder, this is how it reads:

> "The saying is trustworthy: If anyone aspires to the office of overseer, he desires a noble task. 2 Therefore an overseer must be above reproach, the husband of one wife, sober-minded, self-controlled, respectable, hospitable, able to teach, 3 not a drunkard, not violent but gentle, not quarrelsome, not a lover of money. 4 He must manage his own household well, with all dignity keeping his children submissive, 5 for if someone does not know how to manage his own household, how will he care for God's church? 6 He must not be a recent convert, or he may become puffed up with conceit and fall into the condemnation of the devil. 7 Moreover, he must be well thought of by outsiders, so that he may not fall into disgrace, into a snare of the devil."

☐ Do you have a strong sense of calling to shepherd the church and do others see that in you?
☐ Have you read the Bible at least once all the way through in the last five years?
☐ Do you understand that in Mosaic's Eldership model, the emphasis is on shepherding, not decision making? In other words, the traditional "Elder Board" structure is not our model. Our Elders primary job is to *actively shepherd* the people of Mosaic. We are a staff operated, elder shepherded/guided church.

ELDERSHIP DEVELOPMENT

- ☐ Do you 100% agree with Mosaic's Doctrinal Absolutes. Found at http://thisismosaic.org/visit/doctrine/
- ☐ Are you willing to volunteer roughly 8 hours a week at Mosaic Church? (Don't let this scare you too much, it involves things you may already be doing like actively leading in a Missional Community Group, shepherding other leaders, being fully present before and after some weekend gatherings and attending Elder meetings as needed.)
- ☐ Have you been a Covenant Partner in good standing for at least one year? (Check your MCB account if you are not sure.)
- ☐ Are you in a Missional Community Group, preferably leading one?
- ☐ Are you serving in the church already? (Leading an MC is a good example.)
- ☐ Have you been contributing financially to Mosaic Church, regularly, sacrificially and joyfully for at least one year? (Please understand that for those desiring Eldership, we do check the records).
- ☐ Have you listened to the "This Is The Church" series from January 2013 found on thisismosaic.org? http://thisismosaic.org/media/messages/series/this-is-the-church/
- ☐ Are you prepared to read roughly 5,000 pages over the length of our two-year Eldership Development program?
- ☐ Are you prepared to fill out a highly detailed application that will poke into your theology, practice, personal life and faith, family, marriage, your past, and your future? It's a really intrusive application because the Elder role is a really high calling in the church. Your wife will also fill out a questionnaire about you and few questions about herself.
- ☐ Have you read the short version of *Biblical Eldership: Restoring The Eldership To It's Rightful Place In The Church* by Alexander Strauch? This book lays out our understanding of the Shepherding Elder in the church. Many people interested in Eldership find that this is one thing they have not yet done. You'll find it on Amazon. It's only 47 pages and it's available in Kindle Format if you want to go read it right now. Note: If you read the longer version, that is fine also.

Step Two: The Prerequisites to Entering the Elder Development Process

Wow! That's a long list! And that's because we take this calling to *Actively Shepherd* so seriously in the church. If you checked every box here in the affirmative, lets set up a meeting! You can do that by emailing my assistant. In the meantime, I'd like you to buy another book and start working through it. It's called *Gospel Eldership: Equipping A New Generation of Servant Leaders*. By Robert H. Thune You'll find it on Amazon. You'll need to have this read and completed by time you hand in your application (which I will email you after all prerequisites are completed and we have met a second time).

Some people find that they desire to step deeper into Mosaic but do not quite fit the profile of an Elder for one reason or another. If as you looked at this list, you realized, "I don't think I'm supposed to be an Elder, but I do desire to go deeper beyond Covenant Partnership", it's possible that becoming a Deacon might be right for you. Our website has more info on being deacon at Mosaic.

Thank you so much for desiring to go deeper in your journey!

— *Phil Taylor*

Notes for the Implementor:

I want to give you a few notes regarding the prerequisite requirements I've made above. As a reminder, everything set apart within borders is exactly what I send out to participants.

Why do I require reading the whole bible in the last 5 years?

I was talking with an Elder one day at my very first church, and I referenced the book of Lamentations in the Old Testament. He looked at me puzzled and then said "Oh, I haven't spent much time in those kinds of books of the Bible." I asked him if he had read the entire Bible, and he looked incredulously and said "The whole thing?! No, of course not, but I've read all the really important parts." I had this shocking realization that I had an Elder on my team that had not read the entire Bible. An Elder! These are the men that are supposed to be able to rightly handle the Word of God! And he had not even read the whole Bible. I decided on that day that it needed to be a baseline requirement. I added the "in the last five years" bit when I realized that if the last time you read Lamentations was in the Clinton era, you probably don't remember much of it at this point.

Also, a requirement like this acts like a filter keeping lazy men off your team, and it self-selects men who love studying God's Word, like, they do it for fun. Those are the kinds of guys you want on your team.

Did you notice that I said that we check on your giving records?

That's right. When people want to become Deacons or Elders, we actually check to see if they are giving financially. We are not checking tax returns to make sure it's a certain percentage or anything like that. We are just looking to see if you have skin in the game. We want to know that you are giving regularly, sacrificially, and generously. I've only had one guy whose record showed that he wasn't giving anything at all. I was shocked because I knew him well. When I confronted him on it, he said "Oh, I put cash in an

Step Two: The Prerequisites to Entering the Elder Development Process

unmarked envelope every week. My personal conviction is that we are supposed to give in secret so that no one gives you praise for what you contribute financially." I suggested that he might enjoy the tax write off, but he dismissed that saying "that's not why I give." I told him that I respected his conviction, but since no record would ever be created, I would need to ask him once a year or so if he was still giving, and he said that was fine. By the way, we check on this for all existing Elders once a year when we renew Elder Covenants. And we have conversations as needed, which is very infrequent.

Why do I only require the short version of Strauch's Biblical Eldership?

Until very recently, I actually required the full version, but I found that it was more than most Elders really needed. I think people who teach on Eldership, or lead the Eldership Development program at their church should read the full version, but for those who are simply looking to gain a good overview of what we believe on Eldership, the short version does just fine. Also, I wanted to add more heart and character pursuit to the prerequisite section of the process by using Bob Thune's book, "Gospel Eldership." So I rearranged things a bit by dropping the Strauch requirement down to the short version, and then assigning Thune if all other prereq's were met. I've also altered our application to bring it more in line with some of what Thune has done with his excellent set of questions throughout his book. So, some of what you do in Thune will actually show up on your application. If a potential Elder is working on Thune while doing their application, I'm good with that. I think that probably works quite well.

You referenced your Covenant Partnership. Is that a form people fill out?

Yes it is. Since it's required to become an Elder, I thought you'd like to see what it says. I've included it in the appendix of the book.

What happens next?

After I have confirmed that all pre-requisites have been met, I either move them onto Step Three: *The Elder Development Application* right away, or I schedule one more meeting with them (see above) and then send them the application. So, let's move onto Step Three: The Application and Post Application Meeting.

> "All good shepherding finds its root and model in the life and love of God revealed in Jesus Christ. Ultimately, the shepherd we need is Jesus himself."
>
> — THABITI M. ANYABWILE[6]

The Application and Post Application Meeting

I read an article a couple years ago about a utilities worker that discovered a two hundred year old wooden pipe buried deep underground and found that it was still working just fine. Somehow, that pipe survived dozens of advancements in technology and got patched into one new system after another. No one knows exactly when that pipe was laid or how it survived all these years, but sometimes, the response is just to cover it back up and let it keep on doing it's job. That's kind of how I feel about this application. It is an amalgamation of so many different applications that I've found over the years. I know for a fact that it has some questions from the Acts 29 Network Church planter application in it. And I'm pretty sure that the A29 application was based on the original Mars Hill Church application that Mark Driscoll probably wrote in his late twenties. Other questions came from other churches or ministries.

Many of the questions that I wrote or significantly altered came as a result of patterns I kept seeing with people applying to become Elders.

The questions are designed to bring out certain types of information. The problem however, is that you will have a wide variety of people applying. Some will have seminary degrees already under their belts. Others will have a deep calling to the role of Elder, but little theological training beyond sermons and a study bible. I'm convinced that both can become Elders, even though some will need to work harder. Therefore, the questions in some sense are designed to show gaps in understanding that can be addressed during the Eldership Process.

Once I've emailed the application to the potential Elder, I do not chase them down to return it to me. Again, I want them to really *want* to be an Elder.

Ok, let's get on with the application. Since I'm not expecting anyone to fill this out here in this book, I have omitted the spaces between the questions.

On the following pages, you will find exactly what I send out in the application link.

Step Three: The Application and Post Application Meeting

APPLICATION TO BECOME AN ELDER/PASTOR
AT MOSAIC CHURCH

Introduction:

The New Testament tells us that it is good to aspire to the role of Elder/Pastor (1 Tim. 3:1) and gives us clear guidance on the high standards that must be held to if one is to serve with the authority and responsibility of that role. With this in mind, we (the Elders of Mosaic Church) have crafted this application as a way to gauge your understanding of God's Word, your submission to His Spirit and your commitment to His community, the Bride of Christ. We know that words on a page are no substitute for a face-to-face conversation, but they do provide you with the chance to articulate your answers to our questions well, and they give us a chance to read those answers prayerfully.

Here are a few tips as you approach this extensive document.

1. Be very honest. You may find yourself wanting to understate or overstate something to either impress the reader or downplay an issue. That doesn't help anyone and eventually the truth will emerge.

2. When it comes to theology, express your current understanding of things, not what you believe the correct answer is. For example, if you are asked "What is your view of Eschatology?" And you think, "I don't even know what that word means, and I'm not sure I could spell it correctly if asked." Just say that! If you are a little fuzzy on the finer points of the order of Salvation, be honest about that. The goal here is for the current elders to assess where you may be weak and work with you over the next 24 months to address those areas of weakness, whether they are spiritual, theological, pastoral or emotional. We can only do that if we know the areas where you are lacking right now.

3. If you get stuck on a question, answer it briefly. At the end of the day, a short honest answer is better than a long, rambly

answer that essentially says that you don't really know the answer.

4. Remember that the people reading your application are your pastors and your friends. We love you and care for you. We are not out to trick you or trip you up. We want to shepherd you and lead you from one stage of leadership to another. Keep that in the back of your mind as you answer these questions.

Who will be filling out your recommendation forms?

Before you get started on your application, please take a minute to send Phil Taylor the names and email addresses of three people that you would like to fill out a recommendation for you. We will email them a form to fill out. At least one of the names you give should be from Mosaic Church and one should be from outside of Mosaic. Please do not ask pastors/elders or staff at Mosaic to fill out your recommendation form, we already know that we can get their input as needed.

Let's get the legal stuff out of the way first . . .

CONSENT FOR RELEASE OF INFORMATION:

Name: _____

Spouse Name (if married) _____

Address: _____

_____

Email: _____

Phone: _____

I, _____
authorize Mosaic Church to share with the Elders/Pastors the

information disclosed in the testing procedures, questionnaires, and interview process.

I understand that the purpose of discussion among the Elders/Pastors is solely to evaluate my suitability as a potential Elder/Pastor of Mosaic Church and that my information will be treated with sensitivity and confidentiality.

Applicant sign and date: _____

Applicant's spouse sign and date: _____

CONSENT FOR BACKGROUND CHECK:

I, _____
authorize Mosaic Church personnel to conduct background checks on me if one does not already exist in the church database. Additionally, I give permission for the resulting information to be disclosed to the Elders/Pastors of Mosaic Church. (Note: We may send you a separate email with instructions on your background check procedures).

Applicant sign and date: _____

A note about confidentiality and the nature of these questions:

The biblical qualifications have a lot to say about the character of a man's marriage and family. These questions are designed to give us a full picture as we prayerfully consider you as an Elder/Pastor. We are aware that the following questions are personal and very sensitive. Jesus is in the business of redeeming sinners and changing lives, so we do not expect any person's past to be perfectly "clean." Rather, our concern is with unresolved issues from the past or current matters. These issues are sensitive precisely because, unless properly dealt with, they have the power to undermine and destroy you even as you seek to become an Elder/Pastor. Therefore, we ask these questions both for your protection and ours as a church, but especially for those among you to whom you intend to minister. Your answers on this form will only be read by the Elders/Pastors of Mosaic Church. You will be consulted in the event that there is need for further clarification. We appreciate your honesty as you and your spouse (if married) answer these questions.

We'd like to start with several questions about you and your marriage . . .

1. Have you read over the list of pre-requisites and completed any work associated with them such as reading the Bible fully, reading Strauch's short explanation on Biblical Eldership and Thune's study book on Gospel Eldership?

2. How long have you been a part of Mosaic Church?

3. What is your primary campus and which gathering do you typically attend?

4. Have you attended Chapter One yet? When (roughly)?

5. Tell us about your journey into salvation with Jesus and roughly when that took place, along the way, tell us about any churches you have been involved with and how your life has changed after meeting Jesus.

6. Describe your practice of the spiritual disciplines and how you learn from God.

7. Where are you finding opportunities to interact with and develop relationships with non-believers?

8. Tell us about your call into ministry and Eldership.

9. Why do you want to be an Elder?

10. Where are you currently serving and leading?

Step Three: The Application and Post Application Meeting

11. Explain the vision of Mosaic Church as you understand it? Do you find yourself at odds with any aspect or practice of that vision?

12. What do you think Mosaic is doing really well? What do you think Mosaic really needs to improve on?

13. Do you have any unresolved conflict with anyone at Mosaic? If so, please explain?

14. Have you ever been removed from leadership at Mosaic or another church? If so, please explain.

15. Do you have any health concerns that could prevent you from serving faithfully as an Elder/Pastor at Mosaic Church? If so, please explain.

16. Have you ever been charged or convicted of a felony? If yes, indicate dates and please explain.

17. Have you ever been sued personally for any reason? Please describe each situation briefly.

18. Do you or have you used illegal or narcotic drugs or abused prescription medications? If yes, indicate what type, how recently, and in what quantity.

19. Have you ever been involved in any Eastern Religions or occult activities (i.e. tarot cards, Ouija boards, witchcraft, Wicca, new age, etc.)? If yes, please explain.

20. Briefly describe your current financial picture. Include things like debt (credit, school, mortgage etc.), assets and anything else that stands out.

21. Please describe your home life as you grew up? Include things like number of siblings, relationship with your parents, and anything unique that stands out as an important piece of your journey that has shaped who you have become today.

22. Have you ever been a victim of abuse, molestation, or rape? If yes, please share just a little bit about that part of your story.

23. Have you ever sexually abused anyone? If yes, when?

ELDERSHIP DEVELOPMENT

24. Have you ever been sexually involved with a minor, while you yourself were legally considered an adult? If yes, when?

25. To what extent have you been involved with pornography, including cable channels, soft-core porn, internet porn, magazines, etc.?

26. Have you ever had same-sex desires and/or had a same-sex experience? If yes, please explain.

27. Are you now or have you been under a physician's care for mental or emotional treatment? If yes, please explain.

28. Have you ever participated in a 12-Step Program or another type of recovery program for addiction or codependency issues? If yes, please explain.

29. Have you ever been divorced, separated or remarried? If so, please explain in detail the cause and circumstances.

30. Have you ever been unfaithful to your wife in your relationship (emotionally or physically/sexually)? If yes, please explain.

31. How would describe the current health of your marriage (if married)?

32. Describe a time of conflict where the demands of work or ministry put a strain on your marriage, and how you resolved that issue?

33. How do you ensure strength and growth in your marriage?

34. If you have children, explain how that has affected your marriage?

35. Is there anything else about you, your marriage or your family that you believe we should know as we enter this process with you?

36. Have you told the truth in all of the above statements?

Step Three: The Application and Post Application Meeting

Now we would like to ask a few questions about your understanding of theology and other important matters of biblical interpretation . . .

1. Who have been your primary theological teachers or influences? In other words (apart from the Bible and the teaching of Mosaic Church), what authors, theologians (either living or dead), movements, denominations, or schools of thought, podcasts, etc. have most influenced your theology and biblical understanding?

2. Outside of the Bible, what are some of the more theologically-intensive books you have read?

3. What is the gospel? (i.e. theologically speaking, not how you would explain the gospel message to a non-Christian).

4. Please give your view of the scriptures? (Theologically speaking).

5. How do you approach Evangelism and Missional Living?

6. What is our role in saving the lost, and what is God's role?

7. In your own words, how do you understand the doctrine of predestination and what view do you personally hold to on this doctrine? (Please include within your answer: 1) God's sovereignty vs. man's responsibility in regards to salvation, 2) your understanding of free will, 3) who are the elect, 4) why is this doctrine important, and 5) your understanding of the order of salvation).

Note: Please answer all questions and areas listed here with as much detail as you are able to give.

8. How has Adam's sin affected our nature and our ability to choose in regard to good and evil?

9. What is your view of Creation? And what is your view of how mankind (the imago dei) came to be?

10. What is the church and its role today?

11. What is your view and practice with regard to baptism? (I'm looking for things like infant baptism vs. believers baptism, how much water must be used, etc.)

12. What is your view and practice with regard to communion or the Lord's Supper?

13. What is your view of church discipline?

14. What is your view of giving in the church (tithes and offerings)?

15. What is your view of marriage and sexuality? (We are looking for your view on things like same-sex marriage and sexual conduct).

16. What is your view of divorce and remarriage?

17. What is your theology of the Holy Spirit and specifically the gifts of the Holy Spirit? Include here your understanding of things like speaking in tongues, miraculous healing and prophecy.

18. Please describe the gifts of the Holy Spirit that you believe you have.

19. Describe your view of local church government, including the offices, who can/should hold them, and who has final authority for decision making? Talk here about your view of Deacons and Elders.

20. What is your eschatological position (your view of the end times)?

21. Do you hold any theological positions that you believe stand outside the norm at Mosaic Church? Please explain.

22. What are your pet-doctrines, those areas of theology that you just love to keep studying and debating?

Our theology is more than just words on a page. It influences how we live and act and how we shepherd people. Our theology bleeds out into everything we do. With that in mind, let's spend some time on questions related to your pastoral theology. Feel

Step Three: The Application and Post Application Meeting

free to bring in personal stories and experiences as you answer these questions . . .

1. How would you respond pastorally to a couple at church that had just miscarried 9 weeks into pregnancy? What scriptures would you take them to?

2. A college kid is having coffee with you at Axum Coffee, and he wants to know who God is and has a vague idea of this thing called the "Trinity." Please explain how you would pastorally go about talking to this confused person about God and the Trinity.

3. In a follow up the college kid brings in a couple of friends to talk more in depth about who Jesus is. They want biblical answers about who Jesus is and what he did. Again how would you talk with these seekers of truth about Jesus Christ and his works?

4. You are counseling a couple that claim to be Christians, and they are sexually active but not married. They believe they are "married in their hearts." They would like to become Covenant Partners at Mosaic Church. Describe how would you handle this couple, including how you would address the issue of being "married in their hearts"?

5. You are praying with some people after a weekend gathering and a young man says that he would like you to pray for him in regards to an addiction to pornography. What would you do, and how would you on the spot counsel this man?

6. A group of people are talking in the lobby, and they invite you to answer a question they have been trying to figure out. The question they are trying to answer is . . . what role does prayer have in the Christian life if we preach the sovereignty of God at Mosaic? What would be your answer for them?

7. After church one day, you are approached by a crying woman that truly has a broken heart from being convicted of her sin. She simply asks you to tell her the gospel so that she may believe like others in our church. How would you explain the gospel to her?

8. As a follow up to the previous question, how would you then explain to this person how the gospel is involved in the process of sanctification?

9. A student in the church tells you that he has discovered that his dad is having an affair. It is a key family in the church. What course of action would you take?

Now we have a few questions for your wife . . .

1. Tell us about your journey into salvation.

2. What spiritual gifts do you believe you have?

3. How do you currently serve or lead in the church?

4. Explain the vision of Mosaic Church as you understand it? Do you find yourself at odds with any aspect or practice of that vision?

5. Do you hold any doctrinal views or positions that you think may be at odds with the general views of those in leadership at Mosaic?

6. Do you have any unresolved conflict with anyone at Mosaic Church?

7. Do you or your children have any health concerns that could prevent your husband from serving faithfully as an Elder/Pastor at Mosaic Church due to his responsibility to care for his family well? This question refers to both physical and emotional needs (such as severe depression). Please note, these may not disqualify your husband from serving, but they do impact the timing of when he steps into Eldership. Bottom line, we care more about your family than we do about your husband becoming an Elder.

8. Have you ever been unfaithful to your husband in your relationship (emotionally or physically/sexually)? If yes, please explain.

9. Have you ever had same-sex desires and/or had a same-sex experience? If yes, please explain.

Step Three: The Application and Post Application Meeting

10. How would you describe the current health of your marriage?

11. If you have children, explain how having children has affected your marriage?

12. Describe a time of conflict where the demands of work or ministry put a strain on your marriage, and how you resolved that issue?

13. How does your husband ensure strength and growth in your marriage?

14. Can you describe your husbands calling to ministry as you see it?

15. Do you support his desire to be an Elder at Mosaic?

16. Do you believe that your husband is biblically qualified to be an Elder? (See 1 Timothy 3)

17. Can you describe how your husband leads spiritually as the head of the home?

18. Is there anything else about you, your marriage, or your family that you believe we should know as we enter this process with your husband?

19. Have you read all of your husband's answers in his application, and do you believe he has represented things truthfully?

20. Have you told the truth in all of the above statements?

21. Did your husband attempt to influence the way you answered these questions?

Upon completion of this application, please save it as a PDF and then email it directly to Phil Taylor. Electronic Signatures are fine.

Notes For The Implementor:

These questions above are fairly self-explanatory. I've tried to address issues of character, basic theological understanding and how one applies that truth in everyday life. I've gone after hot button issues in the church, and I have not assumed that just because someone wants to be an elder, he has the right views on things. I've made that mistake before. I've also realized through trial and error that sometimes it's the spouse that disqualifies the man from becoming an Elder, so I have increased the number of questions for her over time. While the Elder/Pastor's wife is not an official role or title, there is a baseline of character and maturity that must be present. If an Elders wife is causing problems, I promise you, people will always say *"and she's an Elders wife!?"* Save yourself the trouble and ask the questions up front.

It's worth noting that once again, I do not chase people down once I send them the application. I leave the ball in their court. I want them to truly desire the role of Elder. By giving people helpful and meaningful hoops to jump through, you respectfully give them a chance to decide how fast and how far they want to progress.

Recommendation Form:

You likely noticed the recommendation form I referenced above. It's not complex. I created this list of questions as a way to gain an additional look into the life of the potential Elder. For now, this is simply an Evernote file that gets emailed out by my assistant to the names/email that the Elder Applicant gave me. I bring the results of those recommendation forms to the Post-Application meeting and discuss anything that seems important. Here are the questions on that form.

On the following pages, you will find exactly what I send out in the recommendation form.

Step Three: The Application and Post Application Meeting

Thanks for the effort to fill out this recommendation form for a potential Elder at Mosaic Church. Please take your time and fill this out well. It is critically important that we select only the most qualified to become Elders at Mosaic Church. The simplest thing to do would be to cut and paste these questions into a document of your choosing (Word, google docs, evernote, even the body of an email) and then send it back to me completed.

1. Your Name?
2. Name of the Elder applicant that you are filling this out for?
3. Preferred contact number?
4. City, state, country where you live?
5. What do you do for a living?
6. How old are you?
7. What church do you call home?
8. How do you know the person applying to become an Elder at Mosaic Church?
9. How well do you feel like you know him, and how long have you known him?
10. When you think of the applicant, what words immediately come to mind?
11. Do you believe that the applicant meets the qualifications of an Elder as described in 1 Timothy 3? Here is how that passage reads:

> "The saying is trustworthy: If anyone aspires to the office of overseer, he desires a noble task. 2 Therefore an overseer must be above reproach, the husband of one wife, sober-minded, self-controlled, respectable, hospitable, able to teach, 3 not a drunkard, not violent but gentle, not quarrelsome, not a lover of money. 4 He must manage his own household well, with all dignity keeping his children submissive, 5 for if someone does not know how to manage his own household, how will he care for God's church? 6 He must not be a recent convert, or he may

become puffed up with conceit and fall into the condemnation of the devil. 7 Moreover, he must be well thought of by outsiders, so that he may not fall into disgrace, into a snare of the devil."

12. Does the applicant seem to have an active spiritual life, spending time in the Bible and in prayer regularly?

13. Can you think of anyone that has unresolved conflict with this applicant or his wife?

14. Would you feel proud to call this man one of your Pastors?

15. Do you feel that this applicant has leadership skills? Give an example that you have observed.

16. Knowing that the primary task of an Elder/Pastor is to *actively shepherd the people who go to Mosaic*, does the applicant seem to have a deep care and heart for people?

17. Does the applicant have the ability to explain the Bible to others? Have you personally observed him doing this?

18. How would you describe the applicants marriage and family life?

19. Does the applicant make an intentional effort to build relationships with non-believers?

20. Do you have any concerns at all about the applicant and his readiness to be an Elder at Mosaic?

21. Can you unequivocally recommend this man to the role of Elder/Pastor in the church?

Step Three: The Application and Post Application Meeting

Post-Application Meeting:

So, now that you've seen the application and recommendation questions, let's talk about the Post-Application Meeting with the candidate and his wife. As a review, by the time I'm sitting down for this meeting, the candidate has: 1. Met all the Prerequisites including the initial reading. 2. Had one, maybe two meetings with me personally. 3. Read Gospel Eldership as assigned in the pre-req's doc. 4. Filled out an extensive application. 5. Had three people fill out a recommendation form on him. 6. Had his wife fill out her own application. And now he and his wife sit before me and another Elder, ready to be grilled some more.

The applicants wife absolutely must be there. No exceptions. Her input and even facial expressions are critically important in figuring out the true character and aptitude of the potential Elder. If the Elder candidate shows up without his wife, even though you've made it clear that the meeting had to involve her, I promise you, there is something behind that worth digging into. Someone is hiding something. Politely inform the husband that the meeting will need to be rescheduled. If he is unwilling to have his wife at the meeting, or she is unwilling to attend . . . it's over, plain and simple. You switch into active shepherding mode and serve the couple as best as they will allow.

I like to schedule these meetings adjacent to a weekend gathering because that makes it easier for me to get another Elder to join me. Since I am a staff Elder, I try to bring in a non-staff Elder to balance things out a bit and that usually works out best on a Sunday. If you are in a multi-campus church, it would be best to have an Elder from the potential Elders home campus there, as well as the campus pastor. If you feel that the campus pastor is ready for it, you could certainly hand this meeting over to him instead. I budget two hours for these meetings, but rarely use more than 90 minutes. We conduct the meetings in a quiet and private place as tears are a common occurrence. Don't schedule this at Starbucks! I try have a few water bottles and a tissue box nearby.

As the meeting begins, I set the tone by putting everyone at ease (especially the wife) and keeping the mood upbeat. I like to start off by praising the guys answers on the application. I point out several things that were really great. I look for where his heart showed through really well, and I talk about that for a few minutes. Then, I shift gears and say something like, "So this was a great application (if it actually was), but there are a few things we'd like to go over with you." The other Elder and I have already put a game plan in place. We know our parts. And we spend the next hour or so talking through any concerns we had with the application. I don't have a set list of questions to go over. I just touch on anything that stood out in their application.

In most cases, by the time they get to this place, there are very few major concerns, only minor ones. This makes our job easy. But there are times when I'm going into the meeting knowing that my job here is to let the guy down gently. This requires guiding the meeting very carefully so that he leaves feeling thankful that I loved him enough to be truthful with him.

In some cases, the application brings out a clear difference of theology or practice. This is why it is so important to read these applications very carefully *before* going into the meeting. If all you do is take 10 minutes to skim the application before going into the meeting, you are letting him down, and you are letting your church down. Developing leaders is perhaps the most important thing you do. Take it seriously. You may need to be prepared for a significant theological discussion, or ready to explain a major difference in vision that the application exposed.

One of the men that applied to be an Elder at our church was an incredibly godly older man, but his application reflected an Arminian view of salvation, where as our church is on the Reformed side of that issue. I needed to find out if this was a deeply held belief or simply a lack of understanding. I really loved this guy, and I had a ton of respect for him, but as we discussed this particular point, it became clear that it was a foundational point of doctrine for him. As much as I wanted him on our team, this was a deal breaker for us. He took it well. It's important to know what you are getting yourself into with each meeting. You need be prayed up and prepared.

I generally know before the meeting if we are going to welcome this man into the Elder Development Process or not. If the answer is no, then I try to redirect him to some other part of the church for development. If the answer is yes, I usually spend a few minutes at the end explaining the next steps and then I email or text him (you guessed it) an Evernote file with the Year One schedule for the Elder Development Collective (seriously, I'm not getting paid by Evernote, but I should).

Letting the congregation know about those entering the process:

There are many scriptures in 1 Timothy and Titus that indicate the need for Elders to be extremely well thought of by the congregation. But what is the process for giving people a chance to speak up with concerns about someone being considered for Eldership in the church? We handle it by posting about each person on our website and mentioning it in announcements. It's a great chance to cast some vision from the stage about the need for great leaders in the church and the intensive process we take people through to vet them. In your church, it may make more sense to make an announcement. Whatever method you choose, the goal is to simply give people a chance to speak up before too much time goes by. If you put a man into Eldership and later find out that lots of people knew lots of reasons why he should not have been made an Elder, the failure is on you for not giving people a place to speak up.

And that brings us to Step Four! Year One of the Elder Development Collective.

"Because there is always a need for more shepherds, it is tempting to allow unqualified, unprepared men to assume leadership in the church. This is, however, a time proven formula for failure."

— ALEXANDER STRAUCH[7]

Step Four

Year One of the Elder Development Collective

At long last, we have reached the actual "development" in our Elder Development Process. Finally, we get to start the real training. So does this mean that these guys are now Elders because they filled out the application and endured a few meetings? Nope. We just say that they are "in the Elder Development Collective." We don't call them Elders or Elders in Process—just "in the Elder Development Collective." At the end of Year One, if they make it, they become "Elders-In-Process." I've found that at least 20% don't make it. It's hard work and humans are good liars. Overly busy people don't make it and those with hidden sin patterns are frequently exposed in the first year.

You'll see the schedule below, but first I'll unpack the key components of our monthly meetings, which begin promptly at 7AM for 90 minutes.

The First 15 Minutes Deep Window

This is an important time where I (or another staff member or Elder) spend fifteen minutes going deep into one particular area or initiative at the church. I might have our Student Ministry Pastor explain our philosophy and approach to students, or I might have the Elder in charge of Mosaic Care come and explain how benevolence works, or I might take 15 minutes to talk about the new building project, or our next campus. The point is that I'm starting to treat them like Elders. I'm giving them the inside scoop, and I'm helping them see things at the "Elder level." I do this in the first 15 minutes so that if someone is late, they are not missing the true content of that day. I also do it at the beginning because it gets people there on time. When I send out a reminder email and say that I'll be taking the first 15 minutes to give you a sneak peak at the architecture plans for the new building, they show up on time—trust me!

Theology

We want our men to be trained well in the Word of God and key doctrines. So we have them read Wayne Grudem's *Systematic Theology*. The whole thing. All of it. No cliff notes allowed. It's a bit of gauntlet that we throw down, and we know it. Most months in Year One are spent reading and then discussing a section in Grudem.

Heart and Soul

If we only study theology, we will become lop-sided leaders. So I throw some other key books at them along the way that address leadership, soul care, mission and personality.

Step Four: Year One of the Elder Development Collective

Community

While my focus with these monthly meetings is decidedly on training, I also know that good community does start to develop before and after the meetings, and even during it as we learn to duke it out theologically and still love each other. By the end of the year, we know who is going to talk too much, or care a great deal about certain issues. We know who is going to be super quiet and then come out with one sentence that just blows us all away.

One important lesson I learned was to not let this group get too big. When I had 20 guys in the group, we lost something. It felt like a classroom. When I had 10-12, the whole tone became more friendly and interactive. If I ever have a huge group coming in all at once again, I'll split them into two collectives and meet with them on separate weeks. By the way, you should take attendance each month and track it. If you notice some guys missing a lot, you might need to kick them out.

Below, you will find the information that I send out to all of the men that have been invited to join the Elder Development Collective. This one happens to be from 2014/2015. I've left the dates in for authenticity.

On the following pages, you will find exactly what I send out for Year One of the Elder Development Collective.

ELDER-IN-PROCESS DEVELOPMENT COLLECTIVE
PART ONE | 2014-2015 SCHEDULE

What Is the Elder Development Process For?

Being an Elder/Pastor is not about a title, a task, or climbing some invisible church leadership ladder . . . it's about actively shepherding the church. It's not about how much knowledge we can cram into your head . . . but rather how much character we can build into in your heart and soul. And yet . . . part of being a good shepherd is being a good leader. Caring for the church includes protecting her by being able to handle Scripture well.

We want you to get to the end of your Eldership Development Process and realize that you know Scripture and doctrine better than you ever have before in your entire life. We want your relationship with God to be stronger than it ever has been before. We want you to understand Mosaic's story better than you ever have before and we want your role in that story to be clearer than it ever has been before.

This is a make or break moment for you. We will push you because we love you and because we love the church and we want her to have the best shepherds we can give her.

Buckle up!

The Twelve Months of Part One

Below you will find a breakdown of Part One of the Elder Development Process. All prospective elders will go through Part One in its entirety, but may jump in at any point during the cycle and then simply carry it through until you have done all twelve months.

For example, if you are joining the process in January 2015 –you would go through to the end of this particular cycle in June 2015 and then continue on to the end of end of December 2015 so that

Step Four: Year One of the Elder Development Collective

you have taken part in all 12 components of Part One. This allows us to offer the Elder Development Process continually so that we are continually training up more Elders to lead Mosaic Church.

Times and Locations

In an effort to accommodate the schedule of the working lay-elder, the development collective meets on the third Thursday of the month at 7:00AM at the Mosaic offices. We will finish at 8:30AM. There are occasional exceptions to this rule. I will ask you to arrive on time. I will start on time and end on time because I respect your time.

How Will We Spend Our Gathered Time?

Our First 15 Deep Window will use the first 15 minutes to dig into some aspect of Mosaic's vision and philosophy of ministry. Then, we will get right down to business in discussing the reading material for the month. This will be a guided discussion intended to bring clarity to the content and build community amongst the collective. It is expected that you will arrive having read the whole assignment for that month. Our conversation will focus on the most important pieces of the reading.

Books to Purchase

- *Systematic Theology* | An Introduction to Biblical Doctrine by Wayne Grudem
- *Soul Custody* | Choosing To Care For The One and Only You by Stephen Smith
- *Everyday Church* | Gospel Communities on Mission by Tim Chester and Steve Timmis
- *Strengths Finder* by Tom Rath
- *Absolute Surrender* by Andrew Murray

(*Note:* If you have read any of these books in the last 3 years, you may skim the content for discussion purposes or we can help you select an alternate book.)

ELDERSHIP DEVELOPMENT

What About My Wife?

A key character trait of an elder is that he is leading his family well. We ask that as you journey through these books and discussions, you include your wife and as appropriate even your children in your learning. That does not mean that she needs to read *Systematic Theology* along with you. Just look for opportunities to talk through what you are learning. Let it bleed into everyday conversations. Tell her what you are excited about in your reading, what you are struggling to understand, where you are questioning long-held beliefs and where God is beautifully ruining your soul.

SCHEDULE FOR 2014-2015

August 14, 2014   6PM-Summer BBQ at Phil's house. Bring your family! This BBQ will be a chance for you to spend some time getting to know each other socially before we jump into a crazy schedule over the next year. All of our existing Elders and their families will be there as well.

August 21, 2014   7AM-Discussing Part 1 The Word of God from Systematic Theology. Please read ST-pages 47-140.

First 15 Focus—Setting the stage for the next year.
September 18th, 2014   7AM-Discussing Soul Custody by Stephen Smith. Please read this book in it's entirety.

First 15 Focus—An Elder level look at our philosophy of students and kids ministry (with Pastor Joel Coffman, Next Generation Pastor).
October 16, 2014   7AM-Discussing Part 2 The Doctrine of God from Systematic Theology. Please read ST-pages 141-438.

First 15 Focus—The founding of Mosaic (with Pastor Renaut Van der Riet, founder and Lead Pastor).
November 20, 2014   7AM-Discussing Part 3 The Doctrine of Man from Systematic Theology. Please read ST-pages 439-528.

Step Four: Year One of the Elder Development Collective

First 15 Focus—An Elder level look at Guest Connections at Mosaic (with Carrie Waters, Guest Connection Director).
December 18, 2014   7AM-Discussing Everyday Church | Gospel Communities on Mission by Tim Chester and Steve Timmis. Please read this book in its entirety.

First 15 Focus—An Elder level look at our Missional Community strategy (with Pastor Gabe Forsyth, Discipleship and Missions Pastor).
January 15, 2015   7AM-Discussing Part 4 The Doctrines of Christ and The Holy Spirit from Systematic Theology. Please read ST-pages 529-656.

First 15 Focus—An Elder level look at our Global Missions and Church Planting strategy (with Pastor Gabe Forsyth, Discipleship and Missions Pastor).
February 19, 2015   7AM-Discussing Part 5 The Doctrine of The Application of Redemption from Systematic Theology. Please read ST-pages 657-852.

First 15 Focus—An Elder level look at how benevolence works at Mosaic (with Terry Geter, Operations Director).
March 19, 2015   7AM-Discussing Strengths Finder by Tom Rath (Come prepared to discuss your reading, your results from your online test, and how it all plays into ministry).

First 15 Focus—An Elder level overview of Mosaic's staff (with Phil Taylor, Executive Pastor).
April 16, 2015   7AM-Discussing Part 6 The Doctrine of The Church from Systematic Theology. Please read ST-pages 853-1090.

First 15 Focus—An Elder level look at kids ministry at Mosaic (with Kerri-Ann Hayes, Kids Director).
May 21, 2015   7AM-Discussing Part 7 The Doctrine of The Future from Systematic Theology. Please read ST-pages 1091-1207 (note: this reading assignment also includes a section on historical creeds).

First 15 Focus—An Elder level look at current issues the church is facing (with the appropriate pastor).

June 18, 2015   7AM-Discussing Absolute Surrender by Andrew Murray. Please read this book in it's entirety.

First 15 Focus—An Elder level look at the next couple years at Mosaic (with Phil Taylor, Executive Pastor).

July 16, 2015   6PM-Summer BBQ at Phil's. Bring the Family and meet the newbies joining in for Year One as you are about to start Year Two!

Step Four: Year One of the Elder Development Collective

Notes for the Implementors:

You may be curious about my book choices for Year One. Here are a few thoughts on each.

Systematic Theology-It most closely resembled the theology of our church. You may want to choose a different one. I'd caution you against choosing a way longer one or way shorter one. Calvin's Institutes may be fun for you, but your lay Elders will struggle unnecessarily. On the other end, Stott's "Basic Doctrine" is great for the average believer, but your Elders really ought to be thinking on a different level. Grudem's *Systematic* seems to be just right. By the way, you'll want to create your own notes for discussion with your Elder in Process, but you might not want to re-read all of Grudem if you've done so before. I'd suggest picking up his cheat sheet on Amazon to create your notes and discussion questions quickly.

Soul Custody-I love how Stephen Smith challenges us to embrace *Sabbath Rhythms*. You'd be surprised how many Elder/Pastors never practice a Sabbath. Additionally, the concept of Soul Care has become an increasingly important topic in our church and a key consideration in every decision we make. As such, reading a book on Soul Care is really important for our context because it's key to our vision and mission, but it may not be as important in your setting. This would be an easy one to swap out in your church if there is something you want to fit in.

Everyday Church-I asked our Discipleship and Missions Pastor what book best represented our model for small groups. (We call them Missional Communities). He pointed me to this book, and it has worked out really well. For us, MC's are the lifeblood of our church, so it's important for our Elders to get a book length treatment on what it means to be on mission *in* your community *with* your community. You could easily switch this one out in your church to something that better expresses how you do discipleship.

Strengths Finder-We have all of our staff take the Strengths Finder test and it's been very helpful. Since even our lay Elders function like non-paid staff members, it only made sense to get them on the same page. Plus it's fun to see a test really nail who you are. I encourage the men to discuss this with their families. We list everyone's Top Five in our staff directory.

Absolute Surrender-First of all, Andrew Murray rocks. He might have died 100 years ago, but his stuff is just as relevant as ever. This book is just the kind @$%-kicking men need in every generation. Seriously, it's one of the best books ever written in my view. As an aside, I really like exposing the guys to a classic, long dead writer. It helps us all recognize our tiny place in this thing called the church.

The BBQ's (hosted by our LP or myself) are for all existing elders and those in development, plus their families. This gives us a chance to welcome them into our homes, increasing trust between us. You know someone differently when you've sat on their couch and seen where they live day to day.

Assuming that all has gone well, I move the guys onto Year Two. A few will have dropped out along the way for various reasons, but most move forward. And that brings us to Step Five.

> "Elders who think like missionaries—in their jobs, families, neighborhoods, community responsibilities, schools—think like missionaries in their role in the church."
> — J.R. BRIGGS AND BOB HYATT[8]

Step Five

Year Two of the Elder Development Collective

We have reached Year Two of the Elder Development Process. By this time, your group has narrowed a bit. One guy might have moved to another state for work. Another may have realized that life is just too busy for this right now. And sadly, someone may have disqualified himself for one reason or another. It has been my experience that a good long Eldership Development Process is like the crucible, the refining fire, the magnifying glass on our souls. Anyone can hide sin on an application or in a couple of meetings. It gets harder to hide as you go through a long process. Like Edgar Allen Poe's beating heart, the noise of hidden sin gets louder and louder until eventually it bleeds out somewhere. The leadership microscope often quickens this process.

Regardless of who you started with a year ago, this Year Two group is probably who you will finish with. They will become your next group of Elders (or maybe your first group of Elders). While our church practices "Elders For Life", yours may not. In that case, you'll want to start looking carefully at how these men will fit into your existing Elder team one year from now, and who will roll off as a result. You may choose to invite them into whatever meeting structure you have now, but limit their input until they are full Elders. Our church does not have a cap on the number of Elders on our team, but yours may. In that case, you'll really want to manage that transition well. You are essentially pouring *fresh water* into a *salt water* fish tank. It will be a shock and it will take time for everyone to adjust. Now is the time to start talking about this and begin to drip vision to your existing Elders.

If you find yourself in a larger church, training large groups of Elders, you may consider a Teams (plural) model that I describe briefly here in Step Five, and in greater detail in the appendix of the book in the article titled "Our Elder Teams Model Experiment." That's exactly what it is—an experiment. I have not found any other churches doing this in quite the same way, which either makes us really innovative or aggressively stupid. I don't know yet where we will land. All I know is that the more people you have attending your church, the more shepherding needs there are and the more Elder qualified people you need actively shepherding.

One more note before we take a look at Year Two. I tell people that there are no exceptions to the two-year process, no one gets fast-tracked through. But that's not quite accurate. I do make one un-advertised exception for full time paid staff pastors. Let me give you an example. Last year, we hired a new Worship Pastor. Even though we make no distinction between Elders and Pastors, and therefore train them in the same way, we needed this man to be called Pastor right away (not worship director), and we vetted him pretty carefully before he joined the team. His job required him to step into active shepherding right away (that's a year two thing for the lay elders), and we knew he could handle it. Yet, we didn't want to give him a pass on the process, and truthfully, he needed parts of

Step Five: Year Two of the Elder Development Collective

the process. So we made an arrangement to let him go through both Year One and Year Two at the same exact time. He went to both meetings, read both sets of books and did all the work of both years at the same time with the idea that at the end of one year, he would be considered a full Elder.

Now the reality is that at the end of the year, he still had some work to finish up. I didn't give him a pass. I said "Zack, I can't give you a pass. We'll keep calling you Pastor, but I need to you to finish up this process before we make you a full Elder. Until then, you'll remain an Elder in Process." I think this is a creative solution, and I'd be open to doing it again in unique situations. You should have rules, but you should always be open to breaking them.

Take a look at Year Two below, and I'll catch you at the bottom with some more notes. I've left the actual dates in for authenticity.

On the following pages, you will find exactly what I send out for Year Two of the Elder Development Collective.

ELDER-IN-PROCESS DEVELOPMENT COLLECTIVE
PART TWO | 2016-2017 SCHEDULE

What Is the Elder Development Process For?

Being an Elder/Pastor is not about a title, or a task, or climbing some invisible church leadership ladder . . . it's about shepherding the church. It's not about how much knowledge we can cram into your head . . . but rather how much character we can build into in your heart and soul. We want you to get to the end of your Eldership Development Process and realize that you know Scripture and doctrine better than you ever have before in your entire life. We want your relationship with God to be stronger than it ever has been before. We want you to understand Mosaic's story better than you ever have before and we want your role in that story to be clearer than it ever has been before.

Year One of your Elder Development process was focused largely on book learning and discussion in our monthly gatherings. We did that on purpose because we know that you are busy, and we wanted you to be able to put lots of time into learning before you put lots of time into shepherding. This also gives us a chance to travel with you for a year before stepping into people centered work. With Year One coming to a close, we will now switch gears and begin to call you into *Active Shepherding* and *Targeted Leading*.

This means that we have progressed in how we refer to you. During Year One, we said that you were "in the Elder Development Collective." Were you an Elder? No. Were you an Elder in Process? Not yet. Now that you have finished Year One and are stepping into Year Two with an emphasis on Active Shepherding, we will now call you an "Elder-In-Process." I recognize that many of you have continued in your areas of shepherding throughout Year One. Now, I'll ask you to press into that even more deeply and with a stronger spiritual voice.

Step Five: Year Two of the Elder Development Collective

THE YEAR TWO ELDER DEVELOPMENT SCHEDULE

We will gather six times during the second year (as opposed to monthly during our first year). This is meant to give you more time to step into *Active Shepherding*.

First Gathering

September 8th, 2016 7:00AM

Discussing— "A Praying Life" by Paul Miller.

First 15 Focus—Active Shepherding

The goal of the first gathering is to call all Elders-In-Process into *Active Shepherding* as described below. For our September 8th, 2016 gathering, you should come prepared to talk through where you are already *Actively Shepherding*, or what you are stepping into. The format here is much more casual and relational than our Year One meetings.

The other component to this time together will be discussing Paul Miller's amazing book on prayer. I'll be honest, I don't like most books on prayer. This one was incredible. If we are not praying leaders, we will be dying leaders. It's that simple. This is hard work we are stepping into.

What Is Active Shepherding?

All Elders are called to actively shepherd the people of Mosaic, but that can look very different based on your personality, skill-set, schedule, and existing commitments in ministry. For the volunteer Elder, *active shepherding* will feel like a part time job where you are meeting with people, keeping up with email, prepping for something you are involved in, etc. It will touch every week, and for some, every day. The average volunteer Elder will spend roughly 5-10 hours a week in ministry related activities and will likely be in a leadership role at some point. If you are not already involved in significant active shepherding, please consult with Dave Holland to discover a good place to step in.

Many of our Elders are Missional Community Leader Coaches. This is one of the primary ways to *actively shepherd* and it is a significant commitment. Other Elders *actively shepherd* via Mosaic Care, or counseling, or even Kids Ministry. You may be deeply involved in post-gathering prayer each week. Lots of things could qualify, and we encourage you to utilize your unique design and spiritual gifts to be innovative with your active shepherding. The point is that *active shepherding* is different than faithfully volunteering. An *active shepherd* is providing significant Elder level leadership to a group of people at Mosaic Church and carries with it a different type of spiritual authority. Active Shepherding is the one non-negotiable for all Elders of Mosaic.

What If My Active Shepherding Happens Outside of Mosaic?

Depending on the situation, it may or may not count. The real test is how it touches the people of Mosaic, even if it is not officially a part of Mosaic. For example, let's say that you were deeply involved in helping people think through adoption issues through a local agency, and you find that the vast majority of the people you help go to Mosaic, but not all. This would be a good example of doing *active shepherding* outside of Mosaic Church but with people who attend Mosaic. But let's say you have a heart for Honduras, and every year you took several missions trips there on your own. This is great work to be involved in for sure, but it does not really benefit the people of Mosaic. You are *actively shepherding*, but not at Mosaic. Now, if you were taking a team from Mosaic each time and helping a group of people here catch a vision for Latin American missions and church planting, this starts to look more like active shepherding at Mosaic. If you are not sure if what you do counts, just ask.

Step Five: Year Two of the Elder Development Collective

Post-Gathering Prayer

A few years ago, we launched post-gathering prayer with Elders at all of our weekend gatherings. As you begin your second year, we are asking all of you to serve a few times a month in this capacity. Your wife is welcome to join you in this, and it is an excellent way to serve together. Our goal is to have two Elders available at all gatherings, especially on Sunday mornings, though one is usually sufficient on Thursday night or Sunday night. If you attend the Disney World campus, just check in with the gathering director and show up in the appropriate place for prayer after the announcements. If you attend the Winter Garden campus, the crowds make it a little more complex. Arrive early and go into the sanctuary. Find either the gathering director (who will often be near the sound board) or Phil Taylor, Dave Holland, or Terry Geter, and let them know you are here. We always have a staff back up plan, and then we pull in others as they are available each weekend. This has been the easiest way to do it.

Second Gathering

November 10th, 2016 7:00AM
Discussing—"Sticky Teams" by Larry Osborne and "Church Size Dynamics" (15 page article) by Tim Keller

First 15 Focus—Elder Teams
By this date, you should be settled into your *Active Shepherding* role and functioning well. The goal of the second gathering is to call Elders-In-Process into *Targeted Leading*. For this gathering, we will go in-depth on our Elder Teams model, and discuss suggestions on your particular area of serving. Many of you may already be on a team by this time. In addition to discussing Mosaic's Elder Teams model, we will also discuss *Sticky Teams* by Larry Osborne. It is a teams based leadership classic. Lastly, you will need to read the 15 page article "Church Size Dynamics" by Tim Keller. You will find the article here:

> http://seniorpastorcentral.com/wp-content/uploads/sites/2/2016/04/Tim-Keller-Size-Dynamics.pdf.

ELDERSHIP DEVELOPMENT

If time is short for you, *Sticky Teams* would be a great chance to do an audio book if that is a format that works for you. It's easy to download it on Audible.com and it lasts about 7 hours.

What Are Elder Teams?

Elder Teams are designed to provide task specific, targeted leading opportunities for our Elders and Elders in Process. It is a highly flexible model of leadership designed to respond to the ever-changing needs of a growing church. Teams take on many formats and purposes. For example, if you are an MC coach or deeply involved in Men's Ministry, you'd be on the Elder Discipleship Team. If you were an architect or a land developer, you may be asked to join a Building Team during an expansion phase. Those who preach on the weekends may be on the Elder Teaching Team. If God has gifted you uniquely with the ability to understand and apply doctrine to current situations, you may be asked to join the Doctrine Team. Missions focused Elders could be on a Global Missions Elder Team. Every Elder would find himself on a campus specific Elder Team based on your home campus.

Task specific Elder Teams can be called into existence for a short time or as an ongoing rhythm. Some meet weekly, or monthly or quarterly or on an as-needed basis. An Elder who is actively shepherding would not even need to be on a task specific team at all times. *It is not the decisions we make that define our Eldership, but rather, the Shepherding we engage in.* This is why we can have *Elders For Life* because a person can cycle on and off teams as time permits while continuing to be engaged in *active shepherdin*g as the one constant in the job of the Elder.

Third Gathering

January 12th, 2017 7:00AM

Discussing—"Celebration of Discipline" by Richard Foster

Step Five: Year Two of the Elder Development Collective

First 15 Focus—Pastoral Care
The goal of the third gathering is to deepen your maturity as an Elder and increase your pastoral care skills. Often times, our pastoral care centers around helping people develop healthy rhythms of spiritual discipline. Therefore, Fosters' book has implications in a thousand different situations. As you read this book it will be important to find time to practice some of what you read. Pick one or two the disciplines that you are least comfortable with and dedicate time to them.

Fourth Gathering

March 9th, 2017 7:00AM

Reading—"The Marriage Builder" by Larry Crabb

First 15 Focus—Marriage Care at Mosaic
Marriage care is a huge component of pastoral care. The list of couples needing low level marriage coaching all the way up to full on intensive counseling is never ending. Therefore, Crabb's book on marriage is incredibly helpful in giving you a tool to use with couples. Plus, it will be a great refresher in your own marriages. Single guys should still read the book as you will inevitably end up counseling or leading some married men. If you are married, we are asking you to read this book with your wives.

Fifth Gathering

May 11th, 2017 7:00AM

Discussing—"The Story of Christianity-Part one" by Justo Gonzalez

First 15 Focus—Starting to land the process plane.
The focus of the fourth gathering is to give you a couple months advance notice on how to finish up the Eldership Process.

The church history reading is simply because we believe that leaders in the church need to have a sense of where we came from and how we got here to this place in our shared history. For more than two-thousand years, we have been slowly morphing in the way that we approach our faith and bridge the gap to the culture around us. Some things have stayed the same. Others have been in a constant state of change. Understanding church history helps put all of that in perspective and helps us to know what are truly important things to fight for.

Sixth Gathering

July 13th, 2017 7:00AM

Discussing—"The Story of Christianity-part two" by Justo Gonzalez

Focus—Finishing up the Process
Continuing our focus on Church History, I've simply split up the two volumes into two gatherings. We will also deal with any last remaining questions you have about finishing the process, and we'll walk through the form you will receive on finishing the process and recording your reading progress.

Books to Purchase
- *A Praying Life* by Paul Miller
- *The Marriage Builder* by Larry Crabb (read with your wife)
- *Celebration of Discipline* by Richard Foster
- *The Story of Christianity* (part one and two) by Justo Gonzalez
- *Sticky Teams* by Larry Osborne

Step Five: Year Two of the Elder Development Collective

Notes for the Implementors:

A few words about why I chose these books for Year Two.

A Praying Life: It should go without saying that all Pastors should be men of prayer. And yet, how much have they studied prayer? As I said above, I have found most books on prayer to be unhelpful, except for this one. I believe that a book like this helps our men *actively shepherd.*

The Marriage Builder: This has been the go to book for marriage development that my wife and I have used with couples for roughly 20 years. There are lots of marriage books out there. Some of them are good. What I like about this book is that it very simply addresses one concept, the idea of "oneness." It does not try to be a silver bullet book on marriage, addressing budgeting and chores and sexual technique during pregnancy. It just deals with the idea of "oneness." To me, this book swims upstream and addresses core issues that effect everything else. If all marriage books formed a house, this one would be part of the foundation. Therefore, it's the one I choose to have our guys read (with their wives). When they inevitably step into doing marriage counseling together with couples in need, they have a tool to start with.

Celebration of Discipline: We care a great deal about Soul Care at our church. In fact, during many of our gatherings, we practice the Spiritual Disciplines right in our gatherings for 5-10 minutes. As such, it is important for our Elders to see the theory that goes into that practice. Fosters' book is the basis of our Spiritual Disciplines pursuit.

The Story of Christianity: It is a personal goal of mine to help the church as a whole (leaders to laity) understand and appreciate the role that church history plays in their lives, everyday. So I wanted our men to see where we came from as the church, and a history book is the best way to do that. But why this one? It's so long? Yes, it is long. I wish it were a bit shorter, but the downside of it's length is countered by the free prose of it's writing. This book is called "The Story of Christianity," and that's exactly how it's written—as a story. It feels like you are reading a novel. This is like sticking your dogs heart worm pill inside a hot dog before you feed it to him. It's good for him, and he actually likes it.

How do we land this plane?
As we near the end of Year Two, I begin to prepare the guys for finishing. I warn them that I'll be sending them an online form to fill out, seeking feedback on the process and checking on each individual month of reading. I encourage them to get their reading done, but I make it clear that if they still have some things to finish at the end of Year Two, that's OK. They can take longer—"we'll just keep you as an Elder in Process until you are done." I say several times that if we get to the end, and you still have work to do, I won't just move you forward. I'll wait for to you to finish. By the time they get the Post Development Process Checklist form, they are well aware of what they will see on it. So, with that in mind, let's move on to Step Six.

"What then should characterize a leader with a shepherd's heart? He is willing to give himself to the members of the body of Christ that inhabit his fold. He stands by them no matter what the cost. He knows his sheep. He calls them by name! The sheep know him, they know his voice."

-GENE GETZ[9]

Step Six

The Post Development Process Checklist Form

At the end of Year Two of the Elder Development Collective, I email out this form. I use the forms feature on our Church Community Builder website so that both myself and my assistant get alerted when someone completes the form, and we can easily pull all the answers into a report.

On the following pages, you will find exactly what I send out for the Email and the contents of the linked form.

ELDERSHIP DEVELOPMENT

Hey guys,

It's been such a pleasure to travel with you in the Elder Collective for these last two years. You have all worked so hard, and I appreciate it. This time has not only prepared you well for Elder/Pastor service, but will no doubt impact your effectiveness as a husband and father. Thank you all for taking this seriously! The Bride of Christ is worth it!

As promised, here is THE FORM to fill out, which will help me gauge what work you have remaining to finish in the process. Depending on how much feedback you desire to give, this form could take you anywhere from 15-30 minutes to fill out. I'm leaning on you guys to help me make the next Elder Collective even better.

As a reminder, it's totally fine if you have some reading to finish up. Go ahead and fill out the form now anyway, so that I know roughly how far you are from completion.

I'll be on vacation from June 20th to July 10th, but I look forward to seeing you at the Elders and Family BBQ at my house on July 20th. If you have not already done so, please respond to the E-vite that Tish sent out.

If you have trouble accessing or filling out this form, just let me know.

Thanks for serving Mosaic so well!

Step Six: The Post Development Process Checklist Form

ELDERSHIP PROCESS REVIEW FORM

Allocate 30 minutes to fill out this form.

Men,

You are nearing the end of a two+ year process that has involved an incredible amount of work on your part. Thank you for your diligence and for your desire to serve the church well by becoming a Shepherding Elder at Mosaic. You are almost at the end!

The purpose of this form is two-fold.

> 1. Get a clear and detailed sense of any remaining work for you to finish before you move onto the last two pieces of your Eldership Development Process.
>
> 2. Seek specific and general feedback from you on how the last two years of the process has gone.

What happens next?

If all work is completed, you'll move onto the final check-in with myself and another Elder (we'll require that you bring your wife to this meeting as well). Assuming that this last meeting goes well, you'll be welcomed and recognized as a full Shepherding Elder at Mosaic Church, and you'll be invited onto some of our Elder Teams. We'll pick a weekend at which to welcome you into this high calling. This rite of passage will involve a time to be prayed over by other existing Elders at Mosaic on stage at a gathering.

Thanks for taking time to fill out this form in its entirety. Your feedback will improve the effectiveness of future Elder Development Collectives.

A Note about the definition of "reading"--Throughout this form, you will be asked if you read various books. In most cases, "reading" means that you actually read the whole book or assignment. Sometimes, skimming is appropriate. For example, if two

ELDERSHIP DEVELOPMENT

years ago, you read a 300 page book on Christology, it would be appropriate to skim Grudem's 45 pages on Christology. If you skimmed because you forgot to start the reading until Tuesday, or you just did not enjoy the book, it would be appropriate for you to say that you did not do the reading yet. It's no big deal, you'll just need to finish it before moving forward. I have complete trust in you to understand the difference. If you have any questions about this, or you think your situation is unique, don't hesitate to reach out to Phil.

(Asterisk means it's a required question.)

First Name *

Last Name *

Email *

Mobile Phone *

Birthday *

My primary campus is: *

Prerequisites of applying to become an Elder *

Thinking back more than two years to the prerequisites of the Eldership Process, did you complete the following assignments?

- ☐ I read *Biblical Eldership* by Alexander Strauch (the long or short version both count).
- ☐ I did not read *Biblical Eldership* by Alexander Strauch.
- ☐ I read some of *Biblical Eldership* by Alexander Strauch.

- ☐ I have read the whole Bible at least once.
- ☐ There are parts of the Bible I have never read.

- ☐ I read *Gospel Eldership* by Bob Thune.
- ☐ I did not read *Gospel Eldership* by Bob Thune.
- ☐ I read some of *Gospel Eldership* by Bob Thune.

Step Six: The Post Development Process Checklist Form

Feedback on the Prerequisites.

Did you find reading *Biblical Eldership* helpful as you considered becoming an Elder? How about *Gospel Eldership?* Do you have any other feedback on the "prerequisites" portion of the Eldership Process?

Feedback on the Application Process

Do you have any feedback on the application that you filled out to enter the Eldership Process or the interview that followed it?

Year One of the Eldership Process *

Thinking back to Year One of the Eldership Process, did you complete the following assignments?

- ST refers to *Systematic Theology* by Wayne Grudem.
- See above for a definition of "reading."
- You should have a total of 11 boxes checked. Count it up at the end.

☐ I have read ST-Part 1-"The Word of God."
☐ I have NOT read ST-Part 1-"The Word of God."
☐ I have read SOME OF ST-Part 1-"The Word of God."

☐ I have read *Soul Custody* by Stephen Smith.
☐ I have NOT read *Soul Custody* by Stephen Smith.
☐ I have read SOME OF *Soul Custody* by Stephen Smith.

☐ I have read ST-Part 2-"The Doctrine of God."
☐ I have NOT read ST-Part 2-"The Doctrine of God."
☐ I have read SOME OF ST-Part 2-"The Doctrine of God."

☐ I have read ST-Part 3-"The Doctrine of Man."
☐ I have NOT read ST-Part 3-"The Doctrine of Man."
☐ I have read SOME OF ST-Part 3-"The Doctrine of Man."

☐ I have read *Everyday Church* by Steve Timmis.
☐ I have NOT read *Everyday Church* by Steve Timmis.
☐ I have read SOME OF *Everyday Church* by Steve Timmis.

ELDERSHIP DEVELOPMENT

- ☐ I have read ST-Part 4-"The Doctrines of Christ" and The HS
- ☐ I have NOT read ST-Pt 4-"The Doctrines of Christ" and The HS.
- ☐ I have read SOME OF ST-Pt 4-"The Doctrines of Christ" and HS

- ☐ I have read ST-Pt 5-"The Application of Redemption."
- ☐ I have NOT read ST-Pt 5-"The Application of Redemption."
- ☐ I have read SOME OF ST-Pt 5-"The Application of Redemption."

- ☐ I have read *Strengths Finder* by Tom Rath.
- ☐ I have NOT read *Strengths Finder* by Tom Rath.
- ☐ I have read SOME OF *Strengths Finder* by Tom Rath.

- ☐ I have read ST-Pt 6-"The Doctrine of the Church."
- ☐ I have NOT read ST-Pt 6-"The Doctrine of the Church."
- ☐ I have read SOME OF ST-Pt 6-"The Doctrine of the Church."

- ☐ I have read ST-Pt 7-"The Doctrine of The Future."
- ☐ I have NOT read ST-Pt 7-"The Doctrine of The Future."
- ☐ I have read SOME OF ST-Pt 7-"The Doctrine of The Future."

- ☐ I have read *Absolute Surrender* by Andrew Murray.
- ☐ I have NOT read *Absolute Surrender* by Andrew Murray.
- ☐ I have read SOME OF *Absolute Surrender* by Andrew Murray.

*Did you complete the Strengths Finder Test? And if so, could you please enter your Top 5 below? ***

Feedback on the Year One Assignments

Looking at the list of above of reading assignments, please take a few minutes to give any feedback, positive or negative on the books involved. Please be specific in your Feedback. "I didn't like it" is not a helpful point to make. But a sentence like this would be great: "I felt that (insert name of book) was (insert concern). Something that addressed (insert issue) would have been more helpful in my development." Guys, you are the ones who make the next group better. I want to learn from what went well and what did not, so please take a few minutes on this one.

Step Six: The Post Development Process Checklist Form

Feedback on the Year one "Deep Window" Segment.

On most months, we took 15 minutes at the beginning of our time to look at an area of Mosaic that I wanted you to get a deep window into. (Ex. Global Mission, Student Ministry, New building). Was this time helpful to you? Are there topics you wished we had covered in this time? What would have made this time more effective in your view?

***Year Two of the Eldership Process.* ***

Thinking back over Year Two of the Eldership Process, did you complete the following assignments?

- See above for a definition of "reading".
- You should have a total of 5 boxes checked. Count it up at the end.

☐ I have read *A Praying Life* by Paul Miller.
☐ I have NOT read *A Praying Life* by Paul Miller.
☐ I have read SOME OF *A Praying Life* by Paul Miller.

☐ I have read *Sticky Teams* by Larry Osborne
☐ I have NOT read *Sticky Teams* by Larry Osborne
☐ I have read SOME OF *Sticky Teams* by Larry Osborne

☐ I have read *Celebration of Discipline* by Richard Foster.
☐ I have NOT read *Celebration of Discipline* by Richard Foster.
☐ I have read SOME OF *Celebration of Discipline* by R. Foster.

☐ I have read *Marriage Builder* by Larry Crabb.
☐ I have NOT read *Marriage Builder* by Larry Crabb.
☐ I have read SOME OF *Marriage Builder* by Larry Crabb.

☐ I have read *Story of Christianity* by J. Gonzalez
☐ I have NOT read *Story of Christianity* by J. Gonzalez
☐ I have read SOME OF *Story of Christianity* by J. Gonzalez

Feedback on Year Two Assignments.

Looking at the list of above of reading assignments, please take a few minutes to give any feedback, positive or negative on the books involved. Please be specific in your Feedback. "I didn't like it" is not a helpful point to make. But a sentence like this would be great: "I felt that (insert name of book) was (insert concern). Something that addressed (insert issue) would have been more helpful in my development." Guys, you are the ones that make next years collective even better. I want to learn from what went well and what did not, so please take a few minutes on this one.

Feedback on the whole process.

This is your chance to give any feedback that did not fit into the above opportunities to give it. If your feedback is particularly critical, it may be more effective for us to sit together over coffee. If that is your case, please email tishm@thisismosaic.org to set that up.

Active Shepherding *

Throughout the Eldership Development Process, I tried to repeat this phrase again and again: *The primary job of an Elder/Pastor is to Shepherd the people of Mosaic.*

Looking at your current life, where do you see yourself actively shepherding people who go to Mosaic Church? Please answer this with roles, not locations. In other words, don't say "Oakland Campus," but rather things like, "I'm doing some marriage counseling, and I jump into Post Gathering prayer many weeks. Plus I lead an MC." If you feel like you need help really digging into the best place for you to be actively shepherding, please talk about that below and we'll work with you.

Step Six: The Post Development Process Checklist Form

What are you most excited about now that you are almost done?

You have been on this journey for two years! What are you most excited about as you approach the end of your Eldership Process? Are there areas of the church that you are dying to get into? Issues you hope to bring up? Places you can't wait to serve in?

Do you have more work to do?

If some of your boxes above demonstrate that you have a little more reading to do before completion, please estimate below how many months you think you need. Take into consideration your current work and family schedule and be realistic. Remember, you can still function as an Elder in Process during this time. It just means that we'll hold off on the final steps.

Just for kicks, I thought I'd include the email I sent to my assistant guiding her on how to respond as she receives completed forms from the guys. It's like a *Choose Your Own Adventure* novel. Here it is:

> Tish,
>
> Here is the rough script to follow with the guys as they fill out the forms.
>
> Hi _____,
>
> Thanks for filling out the Elder Review Form. I really appreciate you taking the time to do this!
>
> (If they gave feedback)
>
> Thanks for giving some feedback in your form. Please know that I take every bit of it seriously. I'm always looking to improve our Elder Dev. Program in the next couple of months so this is really helpful.
>
> (If they have no work left to do)
>
> It looks like you are completely finished with all of the work assigned! That's awesome. The next step is for us to get a meeting together with me, you, your wife and one other Elder. Tish will be reaching out to you separately to get that scheduled.
>
> (If they have some work left, books not yet read).
>
> It looks like you've got a small amount of reading left to do. If I don't hear from you, I'll reach back out to you around September to see how things are coming along. Until then, we'll hit the pause button on moving you forward in the process. Don't worry, you are still considered an Elder In Process. Once all the work is done, we'll move onto the next step. Here is a list of your remaining work to finish up based on what you said in your form:

Step Six: The Post Development Process Checklist Form

(list out the items that they have not read, or not read all of).

Again, Thanks for all the work you have put into this process. Don't hesitate to reach out to me with any questions. I look forward to the next step as you become a "Shepherding Elder"!

— Pastor Phil

My assistant then tracks all that data (remember, I'm dealing with a lot of guys here) into a shared file so that I can see where people are. Based on their responses, we figure out what the next step is for them.

If all the work is done:

As you can see above, if all the work is done, I get a meeting scheduled involving myself, one other existing elder, the person coming out of the Elder Process and his wife. The four of us sit down and discuss any remaining concerns and talk through Active Shepherding and serving on Elder Teams. Before that meeting, I have sent him our Eldership Covenant Form to be filled out. Assuming that there are no issues, we will look for a Sunday when we can have this man and his wife on stage to publicly affirm his Eldership at Mosaic.

If he has some work to do still:

We hold off. He continues to function as an Elder-In-Process. If it goes on too long like this, I schedule a meeting to figure out what's happening. Every case is different.

If he never fills out the form:

Of course I resend it first to make sure he got it. But, sometimes, you aren't really surprised. As I write this, I have several guys who went through the whole two-year process, but have not yet finished the workload or even filled out the form. As tempting as it is to just let it slide, I won't do it. You might be thinking: "Phil, what's the big deal? It's just a little reading, he'll get to it." It's actually a much bigger deal than that. You know the phrase about the law serving to point out the sin? (Romans 3:20) Well sometimes, when you give someone work to do in order to become an Elder, they buck against you. Some guys think that they are above the process, but enter it anyway. Then, when I push hard on them actually doing the work, they push back. Do I really want a guy like this on our Elder teams? Is this the right attitude to have when you are actively shepherding in the church? Will these types of guys even actively shepherd? Or just wear the title "Elder" and hope you don't notice that they are not really all that involved.

Some guys will push back saying that the process is too time intensive and that you can't ask busy corporate executives to be doing all this work. My response to that criticism (which I have gotten more than once) is that you have confused our team of shepherds with a board of directors. If what I needed was a board of directors filled with vice presidents and CEO's, doctors and large business owners so that we could sit around and make wise decisions with our massive brains and extensive experience, then I would make the onramp as easy as possible. (By the way, we have all of those types of people on our teams, but not because they have those jobs, but rather, because they love to shepherd). The reality is that I only want the high-powered CEO as an Elder if he is willing to put in the time to shepherd people. If he can't keep up with the reading for two years, he won't be able to keep up with the shepherding as an Elder.

Some guys don't get the work done or fill out the form because they are just lazy. It's hard to quantify laziness, but a form that asks them point blank if they did the work they said they'd do makes it real obvious. By *not* filling out the form, they are avoiding admitting that they did *not* do the work. At some point, I follow up with these guys, becoming the active shepherd in their life, pointing out the sinful pattern that the older translations called "slothfulness." Those conversations are fun.

Step Six: The Post Development Process Checklist Form

So, yes, sometimes doing all the reading is about the principal of the thing. It is very rare that people skip the work they said they'd do out of altruistic reasons. There is usually something else going on. And your job to figure that out and deal with it pastorally. The guys who actually make it to the end get scheduled for that final meeting. So let's talk about that.

"A fitting word of counsel from an elder, kindly spoken, when felt to be from the heart, will touch a conscience that even a sermon cannot reach."

— DAVID DICKSON[10]

Step Seven

The Final Meeting Before Public Affirmation

When the Elder-In-Process has completed all assigned work for certain, I schedule the last meeting with him, his wife, and another Elder. We do this type of meeting at my office for privacy, rather than a restaurant or Starbucks.

At this point, we are really near the end. If big issues are still coming up, or if I still have nagging concerns, then I have not done my job well. Still, this meeting gives me and the Elder-In-Process a chance to talk about any feedback offered. It also gives his wife a chance to bring up any concerns or feedback. In our meeting, we go over the following items, which I have assembled into an Evernote file, which I share with the other Elder doing this final meeting with me.

Items Assembled for Final Meeting:

1. The data from his Elder Review Form, with notes for any concerns or important feedback he offered.
2. His original application from two years ago, with notes on any minor concerns from way back then that we should check back on one last time.
3. Findings from a few areas of engagement in the church:
   - Is his covenant partnership up to date?
   - Are he and his wife still in a Missional Community Group?
   - Is he still serving and leading? (This was actually on the review form they filled out in Step Six.)
   - Does the family giving record demonstrate regularity and sacrifice? (This is exactly what I ask our bookkeeper to check, I don't need exact numbers, just "regularity and sacrifice".)
4. Eldership Covenant Form. We talk through each point on the form, and he hands me his completed and signed form.
5. Projected date for affirming him publicly and any details related to it.

After we go over all these items (again, assuming that things are looking good), we tell the Elder-In-Process that we are ready to welcome him into full Eldership at Mosaic. We close in prayer and we give that prayer a great deal of weight and gravity. In many ways, it's the pre-affirmation. This meeting should be simple and straightforward. You've had two years or more with this guy.

If you find yourself going into this meeting with reservations about making this person an Elder, or even his wife becoming an "Elders wife," I would strongly suggest that you discuss this concern with other Elders first and create a game plan. See if anyone else shares your same fears. 1 Timothy 5:24 tells us that *"The sins of some people are conspicuous, going before them to judgment, but the sins of others appear later."* It is a much bigger deal to remove a full Elder from the team than it is to cut short a guy's process

Step Seven: The Final Meeting Before Public Affirmation

and ask him to either hold off for a bit, or step out altogether. You need to picture yourself standing on the stage in front of your whole church with this man and his wife and saying, "Church, follow this guy in the same way that he follows Christ. Trust him because we do. We've spent two years or more training him up, and we have zero remaining questions." If that image makes you wince even just a little bit, you really need to re-think this person becoming an Elder in your church. Guarding the leadership gate is one of the single most important things you do. I know how problematic it can become when you put the wrong guys on the bus.

> "Do not be hasty in the laying on of hands..."
> — 1 TIM 5:22

Step Eight

Public Affirmation

Finally, it's time to celebrate! This step is pretty straightforward. You pick a date, and you call the guy, his wife and maybe his kids up on stage and welcome him as one of your new Elder/Pastors. You say a few words about the process he's been through, you tell the church a little bit about him and then you gather existing elders to lay hands on him and pray over him. If it makes sense in your church context you might schedule this on the same weekend as some sort of fellowship dinner or picnic so that people can greet him afterwards. At the very least, tell him to hang around after church for as long as possible in the lobby.

If your church is large and has multiple services (we have seven services at our church every weekend in two languages), it will be difficult to get that couple to be at every service. Life will get in the way. So instead, you can either make a video that gets shown at all gatherings, and only pray over him at one. Or you could have multiple new Elders welcomed on the same weekend, but at different gatherings. Our largest campus has six gatherings, so we try to schedule six different new Elders for affirmation, one for each gathering. After praying for that Elder, we would put up on screen pictures of each of the Elders welcomed in that weekend and point people to the website post about all of them. We would put that post in our social media feeds as well.

I'd love to have this followed up by a small reception in a fellowship hall after each gathering for his MC group and other friends and family, just to increase the feeling that this is an important rite of passage. But in our current facilities, we just don't have room.

This public affirmation is also a great chance to tell people who might be interested how to pursue Eldership at your church. Point them to a person, or an email address or a website post. By explaining the process that people go through, it helps your congregation respect these men more. I use a slide on screen that has a picture of a stack of all the books they've read. It's impressive in a scary way.

Conclusion

We have come to the end of the Elder Development Process. We started with a vague interest in becoming an Elder and traveled through multiple steps, all the way from application to affirmation. I don't think for a second that my process is the only way to do it. As Brene Brown says, I'm just *"An experienced mapmaker, and a stumbling traveler"* (216). This is just how we have chosen to do it currently. I'm sure it will morph over the years. Take it, mess with it, make it your own.

My biggest goal in putting this into book form for you is to give you a starting point (and save lots of phone conversations explaining it). I have put at least 150 hours into developing and improving this system over the years. You probably don't have that much time. Lean on my efforts, and make it right for you and your church. If you innovate something that seems to really work, I'd love to hear about it. Leadership development is one of the most important things to get right in your church. If it is a part of your job description, it is the single most important part of it. If you do it right, *it will monopolize your time in the short run and exponentially expand it in the long run.*

Let's get to work.

Appendix One

Covenant Partnership *at* Mosaic Church

What is Covenant Partnership and why do we have it?

Mosaic exists to: *Demonstrate Our Passion For God and His Passion For People*. We do that by *Loving God, Loving People and Serving the World.*

When Jesus Christ called us to Himself for salvation (2 Corinthians 5:17-20), he also called us to the community of faith . . . the church (Ephesians 2:19). When the church is functioning well, we should look like the early church in the book of Acts where resources and daily lives were being shared so freely that the surrounding culture looked in and wondered what on earth was going on in there? We love the church because Jesus loves the church!

As Mosaic has grown to be a community of more than 2,500 people spread out across three campuses at eight services in two languages, the Elders/Pastors have realized the need to bring clarity to who calls Mosaic home and definition to what that actually means. *Covenant* is the biblical language for an agreement or promise. (Genesis 6; 9; 15; Ezekiel 20; Hosea 2; Jeremiah 31; Matthew 26) Our *Partnership Covenant* gives the Elders/Pastors a chance to make some promises to you at the same time that you are making some promises to your church.

What We Believe (Doctrine)

When trying to figure out if you can truly do life with a particular church, it is critically important that you know what that church believes. The following statements represent the most basic biblical and theological beliefs of Mosaic Church. We don't expect everyone to understand every nuance of every word, especially if you are new to the whole *Christ-Following thing*. However, if you see something below that you explicitly reject, we would ask that you gracefully refrain from pursuing Covenant Partnership with Mosaic Church at this time. If you need guidance on a particular area of belief, speak to your Missional Community leader or email a pastor.

- We believe in God the Father, Son and Spirit; creator and sustainer of all things that exist; being eternal and coequal persons. These three are the same in essence having precisely the same nature, attributes and perfections, and are worthy of the same worship and obedience (Genesis 1:26; Psalm 45:6-7; Psalm 110:1; Matthew 3:13-17; Matthew 28:17-20; 1 Corinthians 12:4-6).
- We believe every part of Scripture is God-breathed and useful in showing us truth, exposing our rebellion, correcting our mistakes and training us to live God's way (Psalm 19:7-11; 2 Timothy 3:16; 2 Peter 1:20-21).
- We believe that man was originally created in perfect community with God, free from sin. Man fell into sin by a voluntary act of personal disobedience to the revealed will of God. He lost his spiritual life, and became dead in sins and eternally separated from God (Genesis 6:5; Psalm 51:5; Jeremiah 17:9; Romans 3:23; 5:8, 12-21; 7:18; Ephesians 2:1-3).
- We believe that Jesus Christ died for our sins according to the Scriptures, that he was buried, that he was raised on the third day according to the Scriptures and that the shed blood of Jesus Christ on the cross provides the sole basis for the forgiveness of sins. Therefore, salvation only occurs when

- a person places their faith in the death and resurrection of Christ as the sufficient payment for their sin (John 1:29; 10:1-18; Romans 5:8; 1 Corinthians 15:1-4; 2 Corinthians 5:21; Galatians 1:4; 1 Peter 3:18; Matthew 28:1-20; Mark 16:1-8; Luke 24:1-53; John 1:20-21:25; 1 Corinthians 15:12-34).
- We believe that if you confess with your mouth, "Jesus is Lord," and believe in your heart that God raised him from the dead, you will be saved (John 3:18; 14:6; Acts 4:12; Romans 3:21-26; 1 Timothy 2:5-6).
- We believe that the church is the body of Christ, the community of Christ followers, of which Jesus Christ is the Head. The members are those who have trusted by faith the finished work of Christ. The purpose of the church is to glorify God by demonstrating our passion for Him and His passion for people (Acts 2:42-47; Hebrews 10:23-25; Titus 3:14).
- We believe that we, the community of Christ followers, are called to be like- minded, having the same love, being one in spirit and purpose, doing nothing out of selfish ambition or vain conceit, but in humility considering others better than ourselves. Each of us should look not only to our own interests, but also to the interests of others (Philippians 2:1-11).
- We believe that the God who started this great work in us will keep working in us and bring it to completion on the very day Christ Jesus appears (Philippians 1:6).

Final Authority for Matters of Belief and Conduct

This statement of faith does not exhaust the extent of our beliefs. The Bible itself, as the inspired and infallible Word of God that speaks with final authority concerning truth, morality, and the proper conduct of mankind, is the sole and final source of all that we believe. For purposes of Mosaic Church's faith, doctrine, practice, policy, and discipline, our Elder/Pastor Team is Mosaic's final interpretive authority on the Bible's meaning and application.

The Elders/Pastors Covenant with you to . . .
- Appoint Elders and Deacons (including staff members) according to the scriptures (1 Timothy 3:1-13; Titus 1:5-9; 1 Peter 5:1-4).
- Pursue the Spirit's guidance as we lead the church and steward her resources (Acts 20:28; 1 Peter 5:1-4).
- To care for the church by shepherding her well, praying for her, teaching the Scriptures, equipping people for ministry, protecting her from false teachers and lovingly exercising correction when necessary (Matthew 7:15; 18:15-20; 28:16-20; Ephesians 4:11-16; James 5:14; 1 Peter 5:1-4; Acts 20:27-31; 1 Corinthians 5; Galatians 6:1; 1 Timothy 1:3-7; 4:16; 2 Timothy 4:1-5; 1 John 4:1).
- To lead by example in following all that is found in the Partnership Covenant that you sign (Philippians 3:17; 1 Timothy 4:12; Titus 2:7-8; 1 Peter 5:3).
- You Covenant with the church to . . .
- Read Scripture regularly and prayerfully submit to its authority in your life (Psalm 119; Acts 17:11; 2 Timothy 3:14-17; 2 Peter 1:19-21).
- Follow the commands of Scripture and example of Jesus by taking part in the Sacraments of the church such as communion and baptism *after* your profession of faith. (Acts 2:38; 10:48; Romans 6:4; 1 Corinthians 11:24-27).
- Take part in our weekend worship gatherings *and more importantly* . . . to be active in a Missional Community during the week (Acts 2:42-47; Hebrews 10:23-25). NOTE: You can join a missional community by filling out the form found here: www.thisismosaic.org/community
- Serve in some way in the church (such as Mosaic Kids, Hospitality, Bands, Tech, etc.) (Titus 3:14). NOTE: You can

Appendix One: Covenant Partnership at Mosaic Church

- start serving by filling out the form found here: www.thisismosaic.org/serve
- Carefully oversee the resources God has given you and give financially to the work of Mosaic Church *regularly, sacrificially, and cheerfully* (Matthew 25:14-20; Romans 12:1-2; 2 Corinthians 8-9; 1 Peter 4:10-11). NOTE: You can give financially to the church via our public website, MCB and depositing checks and cash in the boxes at the back of the auditorium. You can also mail checks to: Mosaic Church | 608 W. Oakland Ave. | Oakland, FL | 34760
- Submit to the discipline of God within the church when other Christ-Followers and our Elders/Pastors approach you biblically with concerns and follow the biblical guidelines when you yourself need to approach others who are in sin, avoiding gossip at all costs (Psalm 141:5; Matthew 18:15-20; 1 Corinthians 5:9- 13; Hebrews 12:5-11).

How do I become an official Covenant Partner?

- Fill out the form on the next page and mail it to our Elders/Pastors at:
  Mosaic Church | 608 W. Oakland Ave. | Oakland, FL | 34760
- Or scan it and email it to covenant@thisismosaic.org
- Or complete the digital version of this covenant at www.thisismosaic.org/covenant

What happens after I fill out the form?

Because we truly care for you and because we take Covenant Partnership very seriously, the Elders/Pastors will ensure that you are currently involved in a missional community, currently serving somewhere in the church and currently contributing financially to the mission and vision of Mosaic Church. If you are in process on any of those items, briefly explain the situation and an Elder/Pastor or Deacon will follow up with you.

Once everything is confirmed we will change your designation on MCB to "covenant partner" and let you know via email, MCB mail or regular mail that your covenant partnership is complete and approved. We will also let your Missional Community group leaders know so that they can celebrate with you! There are no discounts on oil changes or special handshakes that only partners learn. Covenant Partnership at Mosaic is a statement of agreement with and excitement about our mission and vision in this world. It is a way of stating officially and unequivocally "I am on board! I'm with you! I'm all in!" We can't wait to see how God uses you to impact the journey of Mosaic Church.

COVENANT PARTNERSHIP FORM @ MOSAIC CHURCH

Full Name _____

Street Address/P.O. Box_____

City _____State_____ Zip Code_____

Best Phone # _____

Email Address_____

Marital Status _____ Birth Date_____

Do you have an MCB account? _____

What Campus do you worship at?_____

Previous Church membership(s) in the last three years (Name, City and State)_____

_____

Do you consider yourself a follower of Jesus Christ and the teachings of the Bible? _____

Appendix One: Covenant Partnership at Mosaic Church

Please describe your faith journey on a separate sheet or on the back of this page.

Have you been baptized in water *after* your profession of faith in Jesus Christ? Please list when and where: _____

_____

(Let us know if you need to be baptized and we'll schedule you for the next baptism weekend).

Have you read Mosaic's statement of belief and will you agree to support it? _____

Are you in a Missional Community at Mosaic Church? _____

If you are not currently in a group, we will help you find one. Please fill out the form found at www.thisismosaic.org/community. If yes, please list group by leader & location: _____

_____

Are you currently and regularly giving financially to Mosaic Church? (Remember that you can give via our website as well as MCB and by putting checks directly in the tithe boxes at the back of the room.) _____

List the areas in which you serve within the church:

_____

_____

Are you willing to place yourself under the spiritual authority of the Pastors/Elders of Mosaic? _____

Signature _____

Date _____

Last edited on December 9th, 2013

Appendix Two

Elders/Pastors Covenant *with* Mosaic Church

It is a simple fact of life . . . leaders are held to a different standard. Ephesians 5 demonstrates this so well when Paul takes three verses to explain what is asked of wives in a marriage and nine verses to explain the standard that husbands are held to. Being in a position of headship . . . leadership . . . is just different. It is a high calling that cannot be ventured into lightly.

As Elders/Pastors at Mosaic we want to be men that others can look to and say "I aspire to be like him, because he aspires to be like Jesus and Jesus loves His church." We are first and foremost shepherds actively caring for the flock that God has called us to. Secondly, we each bring different gifts to the body that, when used well, carry greater weight due to our positions of spiritual authority within the church. In other words, when you preach, you are not just a teacher, you are a teaching Elder; when you pray over someone, you are praying *as an Elder of the church.*

Part of what brings legitimacy to all that we do as Elders/Pastors is a clear understanding of the covenant promises we have made to each other and the church at large. This Elder/Pastor Covenant is intended to define clearly for others and ourselves how we have agreed to live.

ELDERSHIP DEVELOPMENT

I covenant with the body of Mosaic Church and my fellow Elders/Pastors to set the example by upholding all that we ask of those who embrace Mosaic's Partnership Covenant. The key points are:

- Read Scripture regularly and prayerfully submit to its authority in your life (Psalm 119; Acts 17:11; 2 Timothy 3:14-17; 2 Peter 1:19-21).
- Follow the commands of Scripture and example of Jesus by taking part in the Sacraments of the church such as communion and baptism *after* your profession of faith. (Acts 2:38; 10:48; Romans 6:4; 1 Corinthians 11:24-27).
- Take part in our weekend worship gatherings *and more importantly* – be active in a Missional Community during the week (Acts 2:42-47; Hebrews 10:23-25).

Note: You can join a missional community by filling out the form found here: www.thisismosaic.org/community

- Serve in some way in the church (such as Mosaic Kids, Hospitality, Bands, Tech, etc.) (Titus 3:14). NOTE: You can start serving by filling out the form found here: www.thisismosaic.org/serve
- Carefully oversee the resources God has given you and give financially to the work of Mosaic Church *regularly, sacrificially, and cheerfully* (Matthew 25:14-20; Romans 12:1-2; 2 Corinthians 8-9; 1 Peter 4:10-11).
- Submit to the discipline of God within the church when other Christ-Followers and our Elders/Pastors approach you biblically with concerns and follow the biblical guidelines when you yourself need to approach others who are in sin, avoiding gossip at all costs (Psalm 141:5; Matthew 18:15-20; 1 Corinthians 5:9- 13; Hebrews 12:5-11).

Appendix Two: Elders/Pastors Covenant with Mosaic Church

In addition to these things that we ask of our Covenant Partners, I covenant to keep the promises that the Elders/Pastors have made to those who have agreed to Mosaic's Partnership Covenant. The key points are:

- Appoint Elders and Deacons (including staff members) according to the Scriptures (1 Timothy 3:1-13; Titus 1:5-9; 1 Peter 5:1-4).
- Pursue the Spirit's guidance as we lead the church and steward her resources (Acts 20:28; 1 Peter 5:1-4).
- To care for the church by shepherding her well, praying for her, teaching the Scriptures, equipping people for ministry, protecting her from false teachers and lovingly exercising correction when necessary (Matthew 7:15; 18:15-20; 28:16-20; Ephesians 4:11-16; James 5:14; 1 Peter 5:1-4; Acts 20:27-31; 1 Corinthians 5; Galatians 6:1; 1 Timothy 1:3-7; 4:16; 2 Timothy 4:1-5; 1 John 4:1).
- To lead by example in following all that is found in the Partnership Covenant that you sign (Philippians 3:17; 1 Timothy 4:12; Titus 2:7-8; 1 Peter 5:3).

In addition to this baseline that we all live by, there are a few practical matters that are worth spelling out. I covenant to be available for the shepherding work of the church in the following ways . . .

- Attend the appropriate Elders/Pastors meetings whenever possible.
- Be attentive to communication tools (such as e-mail) amongst the Elders/Pastors in an effort to move things forward and remain aware of the issues and needs of our community.
- Lead a Missional Community and coach several Missional Community Leaders.
- Be willing to alter my work schedule on rare occasions for the sake of the church.

ELDERSHIP DEVELOPMENT

- Be physically present in the lobby before and after the weekend gathering that I attend by arriving early and staying late, intentionally engaging people I don't know, being available to pray over people that have requested that of the Elders/Pastors, serving communion.
- Be available on occasion for Chapter 1 and Chapter 2 classes.
- Recognize that the duties of being an Elder/Pastor require a minimum of 8 hours a week on average. (Breakdown: Weekend Gatherings-2-3 hours, Leading a Missional Community-2-4 hours, Coaching MC Leaders-2 hours, Elder meetings and other shepherding needs-2-4 hours.)
- I will set the example with my tithes and offering by giving to Mosaic Church regularly, sacrificially and joyfully.
- Vigorously debate issues within an Elders/Pastors meeting while vigorously supporting decisions outside of those meetings.
- Assume the best (1 Cor. 13) of my fellow Elders/Pastors when faced with a potential offense, being careful to follow Matthew 19 in resolving conflict.
- If and when a congregant attempts to gossip about a fellow Elder/Pastor, I will not give a listening ear and so stir up dissension, but immediately point him/her to Matthew 19.

I will believe in and support the doctrine associated with the Partnership Covenant as a statement of basic belief. Additionally, I will agree to support the statement on "Doctrinal Convictions" publicly, being careful not to teach against it even if there are minor areas where I myself disagree.

If at any point in the future, my doctrinal beliefs change, I will inform my fellow Elders/Pastors and submit to their recommendations for my future on the team.

Name: _____

Date: _____

Appendix Three

Our Elder Teams Experiment

This is a document we created at Mosaic Church to guide our experiment with Elder Teams (as opposed to just one Elder Team singular). This is a very new thing for us and I have no idea how it will go over the coming years, but I believe in letting others in on our learning process. If you are reading this long after 2017, check BackstagePastors.org to see a progress report.

Elder Teams at Mosaic

We are first and foremost shepherds, everything else is extra.

Since Mosaic's inception, our day-to-day working model of church leadership has been *Elder guided and Deacon operated*. We may not have expressed it that way in the early days, but that's really what we were. We may not have called all of our pastors *elders* or all of our elders *pastors*, but that's what they were becoming. We may not have recognized our non-pastoral staff as deacons, but that's how they were functioning. We have been working hard at calling our current leaders to a higher standard complete with biblical titles, while simultaneously creating opportunities and systems to develop new leaders . . . all in an effort to become a church marked by healthy leadership that loves to shepherd the people well. We've added things like post-gathering prayer, MC coaches, and a higher pastoral presence at all campuses. We've taken things that were already happening, like benevolence and counseling and added a stronger pastoral touch and oversight to it. Again, **we are first and foremost shepherds, everything else is extra.**

And yet, we are called to do other things as Elders. We teach, we lead, we guard doctrine, we set direction for the future. In short, we guard the gospel, and we protect the church. When our current Elder Team was first called together by Pastor Renaut, we were less than one hundred people. We are now 2500 people on a weekend (soon we will have roughly one elder per hundred). As we welcome new Elders into our ranks growing from 5 elders in 2013 to twenty-five Elders in 2017, it is time to let our current system of *all* Elders meeting monthly on everything pass away. Remember, **we are first and foremost shepherds, everything else is extra.**

In addition to our ongoing active shepherding, we are implementing our *Elder Teams Model* where each Elder can be on a few teams that are task specific. For example, if you are an MC coach, or deeply involved in Men's Ministry, you'd be on the Elder Discipleship Team. If you were an architect, or a land developer, you may be asked to join a Big Projects Team during an expansion phase. Those who preach on the weekends may be on the Elder Communicators Team. If God has gifted you uniquely with the ability to understand and apply doctrine to current cultural situations, you may be on the Doctrine Team. Task specific Elder Teams can be called into existence for a short time or a long time. Some will meet weekly, or monthly or quarterly or on an as-needed basis. An Elder who is actively shepherding would not even need to be on additional teams at all times. He could simply shepherd well in the day to day of ministry.

A current list of teams follows. Each team will have a point person determined by the team, or assigned by the Directional Elders Team. Teams that are currently active will provide a monthly report to Phil Taylor to share with the Directional Elder Team so that there is always one team that is aware of the big picture of all the work that our Elders are leading in the church. This also helps ensure that we are moving forward in one direction. The Directional

Appendix Three: Our Elder Teams Experiment

Team may also ask Elder Teams engaged in current work to provide a summary report to Phil Taylor roughly 10 days before the quarterly All Elder meetings to be shared with the whole body of Elders.

All teams will do an internal review once a year (roughly February) to determine the effectiveness of their team makeup. Teams can re-evaluate throughout the year, but February's review provides for one guaranteed conversation. At that time, each team can decide if they need different skill-sets, personality types, or availability based on whatever projects they are engaged in. The Directional Team will assist other teams as needed.

- **Doctrine Team**-Designed to be called into action to respond to doctrinal questions arising from within our church or culture. Ex. A group of highly charismatic people begin holy laughter during our services. Activate the Doctrine team to assemble a quick response. Or, the church needs to know where we stand on LGBTQ issues after a Supreme Court decision, the doctrine team responds lovingly with written biblical teaching and care.
- **Communicators Team**-This group does the primary communication at the weekend gatherings. They demonstrate a unique gifting at teaching God's Word. It is understood that all Elders should be teaching in one way or another via an MC or Kid's Min, or Equipping class, etc. This team is specifically for those integrally involved in weekend gathering communication.
- **Missions and Church Planting Team**-This team works closely with the Missions Pastor to guide decisions and do research on those we support globally and locally and then aid in our ongoing personal support through connections and visits.
- **Discipleship/MC Leaders Team**-These guys have key roles in Discipleship throughout the church, such as coaching and demographic specific ministry. Ex. If you coach MC leaders, you would be on this team.

ELDERSHIP DEVELOPMENT

- **Benevolence Team**-Elders stepping into some of the harder benevolence situations. For example, let's say that a family's house burned down, that requires more pastoral care than someone needing some help getting groceries.
- **Big Projects Team**-Building facilities, launching something major.
- **HR/Finance Team**-Works with Terry Geter in assessing Human Resources and budgetary issues. Provides a checks and balances function.
- **Latino Campus Team**-Elders who serve significantly with the Latino Campus.
- **WDW Campus Team**-Elders who serve significantly with the WDW Campus.
- **Elder On-boarding Team**-As men express a desire to become Elders, this team helps them through the process through assessments and potentially coaching.
- **Elder Level Church Discipline Team**-When outright sin is exposed in someones life and there is a lack of repentance, this team will step in to handle these difficult pastoral situations with the goal of restoration.
- **New Campus Development Team**-As we start new campuses, this group will assist in research and development.
- **Post Gathering Prayer Team**-Praying after the gatherings. Frontline shepherding at it's best. Every Elder must be available for this team. It's the one non-negotiable unless you are the primary communicator at your campus.
- **Directional Team**-Charts a course for the future of the church. Has oversight over the other teams. Provides accountability and guidance for LP and XP. See below for more.

Directional Team

The Directional Elder Team is unique and is therefore called out separately here. This is the group of Elders that are meeting monthly

Appendix Three: Our Elder Teams Experiment

to influence and guide the overall direction of the church and provide counsel and covering to our Lead Pastor and Executive Pastor. In the past, the Directional Team was simply the full Elder team meeting every 4-6 weeks. As our Elder count goes from 10 to 25, it becomes necessary to adjust the way this team functions as having 25 people sitting around a room making decisions is a recipe for disaster. Because the Directional Team carries with it a different level of decision making responsibility, we have adopted the following guidelines.

- Its total number will not exceed eleven or go below five.
- It will always contain an odd number of participants, weighted towards non-staff. Ex. If we have 5 on the team, three will be non-staff. If we have 7 on the team, 4 will be non-staff.
- The Lead Pastor and Executive Pastor will always remain on this team due to their unique roles in the church. In the event that one or both roles are vacated, or either is incapacitated, the Staff Elders serving in similar temporary roles should step onto this team during the absence.
- All other participants have the ability to serve continually and without forced rotations off the team. As with all other teams, the Directional Elders will reassess the makeup and effectiveness of the team each February. If they are recommending replacements or new additions to their team from the existing Elders, they will report those suggestions to all Elders for casual input and feedback. If there are no concerns voiced, the changes will take effect after two weeks.
- In an effort to maintain continuity, we will start with seven elders and we are asking for an initial two-year commitment from them. Any time a new Elder joins the Directional Team, we will ask him to be open to serving for two years, even though the team is re-evaluated each year.
- One must be a fully affirmed Elder before becoming eligible for this team.

ELDERSHIP DEVELOPMENT

- The Directional Team will determine participants for new teams with counsel welcomed from all via email or in writing at our first quarterly all-elder meeting of the calendar year. Teams that are determined purely by function need no approval. For example, if you begin coaching MC leaders, you automatically join that team. No discussion needed.
- In cases of death, long-term illness or Elder disqualification, replacements will be handled via email or at the nearest All-Elder meeting, or specially called meeting.
- The minutes of the Directional Team meetings will be shared with *all* Elders within seven business days of the meeting via the "All Elder Communication" File in Evernote. It is your responsibility to check it.
- Any Elder may ask any Directional Team Elders for clarification on something discussed in a meeting as reflected in the notes.
- Being on the Directional Team does not replace *active shepherding*.
- The Directional Team, in essence, provides direction and leadership to the full-counsel of Elders and ensures that all Elders are kept well informed through quarterly meetings and regular communication.
- Very significant decisions will be brought to the full counsel of Elders by the Directional Team for discussion and input, and where needed, a vote. Ex. Hiring an new LP or XP; borrowing more than one million dollars, purchasing land, changing the bylaws or removing an Elder. All such decisions will be brought to the All Elder Quarterly meeting, or to a specially called meeting where a simple majority is physically or virtually present, or in some cases may simply be handled via email.
- The Directional Team will meet monthly on Wednesday mornings at 7AM unless decided otherwise. Meetings will

be scheduled at least 3 months out to allow for proper planning. Team members should plan work and personal travel around these meetings, and be willing to FaceTime in when missing a meeting is unavoidable.

A few other things related to our Teams Model:

Conflict Resolution: If a member of a team has a concern about something going on within their team, and they have already followed Matthew 18 in conflict resolution, they may bring that concern to the Directional team for discussion and resolution. The way to do this is to email Phil Taylor who will then add it to the agenda of the next Directional Team meeting.

Experimental Nature: As we step into this new model, there is an inherent danger that it simply will not work out in practice. We expect the need to make adjustments to it, but we need to be open to trashing it altogether if it fails. The original Directional Team decided on a two year trial period with significant reviews at the one year mark (January 2018) and two year mark (January 2019) by the original Directional Team as it existed in August 2016 (for consistency sake). That team will evaluate its effectiveness at creating better pathways for shepherding and leading our people well along with any input provided by other Elders.

Internal Consultants: There will be times when an Elder who has a particular skill set or experience will be called upon to provide consultation by another team. This is normal and helpful and does require any official actions.

All Elders Meeting Frequency:

Quarterly

All Elders Communication:

We utilize a shared Evernote File maintained by Phil Taylor. By sending him updates, he will ensure that they are posted in the All

Elders Communication File. This method may not work long term, but it gets us started. We can re-evaluate after a year so as not to over build our systems.

Individual Team Meeting Frequency:

As needed.

Appendix Four

How to get everything you see here in a word file.

You have seen a lot of resources in this book. If you are like me, you might be thinking, "Gosh, I wish I could get all these files in an editable format." Good news! I am very happy to share them with you. Simply send an email to backstagepastors@gmail.com and I'll give you all of it in word format. All I will ask is that you do not re-publish it, or post it on your blog etc.

Endnotes

1. *Gospel Eldership.* Robert Thune Pg 1
2. One notable exception is "The Elder Training Handbook" by Carey Green
3. For a more complete explanation of our Elder Teams Model, check out the appropriate Appendix.
4. *Church Elders.* Jeremy Rinne, Pg 20
5. thisismosaic.org
6. *Finding Faithful Elders and Deacons.* Thabiti Anyabwile, Pg 49
7. *Biblical Eldership.* Alexander Strauch, Pg 68
8. *Eldership and the Mission of God.* J.R. Briggs and Bob Hyatt, Pg. 29
9. *Elders and Leaders.* Gene Getz, Pg. 152
10. *The Elder And His Work,* David Dickson, Pg. 67

Bibliography and Resources on Biblical Eldership

Thune, Robert. *Gospel Eldership-Equipping a New Generation of Servant Leaders.* Greensboro, NC: New Growth Press, 2016 [Great study guide.]

Strauch, Alexander. *Biblical Eldership-An Urgent Call To Restore Biblical Church Leadership.* Colorado Springs: Lewis & Roth Publishers, 1995 [This is the longer version of Strauch's book. Great for people leading the Elder Development program in a church.]

Strauch, Alexander. *Biblical Eldership-Restoring The Eldership To It's Rightful Place In The Church.* Colorado Springs: Lewis & Roth Publishers, 1997 [This is the shorter version of Strauch's book. The best short explanation of Eldership I know of.]

Green, Carey. *The Elder Training Handbook-An Assessment and Training Tool for the Church.* Green House Publishing, 2010 [If you think my system is too long, consider this one.]

Rinne, Jeremy. *Church Elders-How to Shepherd God's People Like Jesus.* Wheaton, IL: Crossway, 2014 [Small book overview]

Anyabwile, Thabiti M. *Finding Faithful Elders and Deacons.* Wheaton, IL: Crossway, 2012

Briggs, J.R. & Hyatt, Bob. *Eldership and the Mission of God-Equipping Teams For Faithful Church Leadership.* Downer's Grove, IL: Intervarsity Press, 2015 [Very Missionally focused and culturally aware.]

Getz, Gene. *Elders and Leaders-God's Plan for Leading the Church*. Chicago, Moody Publishers, 2003 [Classic Gene Getz, exegetical approach. A good alternative to Strauch's longer book.]

Dickson, David. *The Elder and His Work*. Phillipsburg, NJ, P&R Publishing, 2004 [Written in a Presbyterian context.]

Newton, Phil A. & Schmucker, Matt. *Elders in the Life of the Church-Rediscovering the Biblical Model for Church Leadership*. Grand Rapids, MI: Kregel, 2014 [Written in a Baptist Context.]

Evans, Daniel & Godwin, Joseph JR. *Elder Governance-Insights into Making the Transition*. Eugene, OR: Resource Publications, 2011 [Focuses on churches making the shift to Elders.]

Anderson, Lynn. *They Smell Like Sheep*. West Monroe, LA: Howard Publishing, 1997 [Emphasizes the shepherding role of Elders.]

About the Author

Phil is a graduate of Cairn University and Dallas Theological Seminary and has served the church for over twenty years. He is passionate about bringing vision into reality and has spent the last twelve years serving alongside of gifted communicator-visionary *Lead Pastors* of Acts 29 Network churches in New York and Florida where he now serves as the Executive Pastor of Leadership and Development at Mosaic, a multi-site church in West Orlando and at Walt Disney World. (www.thisismosaic.org) Phil loves reading, researching, writing, running and kayaking. He has been married to Aimee since 2002. They live west of Orlando, Florida with their three children and one cat.

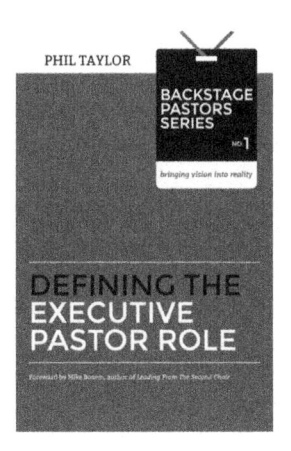

Phil's first book *Defining The Executive Pastor Role* is available on Amazon.com in English and Spanish in both paperback and Kindle formats.

Contacting the Author

For speaking, consulting or coaching requests, please email: backstagepastors@gmail.com

Social Media

Twitter: @philtaylorxp
Instagram: @philtaylorxp
Facebook: facebook.com/philtaylorxp

For articles and additional information from the author, such as upcoming speaking engagements or new books, visit www.backstagepastors.com.

Made in the USA
Monee, IL
09 November 2019